ANGRY TÍAS:

Cruelty and Compassion on the U.S.-Mexico Border

by Daniel Blue Tyx

Angry Tías

Published with the support of UltraViolet. Visit WeAreUltraViolet.org for more information.

Published in the United States by Strong Arm Press, 2019

www.strongarmpress.com

ISBN-13: 978-1-947492-34-9

Vilma   Aracely   López   Juc   de   Coc   and   her   11-year-old   son
Vilma was forced to flee her village in Guatemala after her husband was brutally murdered. Her only goal was to save her son from suffering the same fate. Upon being detained by Border Patrol agents, her son was taken away from her. She hasn't seen her son since they were separated on May 22, 2018.

> --from "Emergency Request for Precautionary Measures Pursuant to Article 25 of the Rules of Procedure of the Inter-American Commission on Human Rights on Behalf of Parents Systematically Separated from their Parents at the United States-Mexico Border," submitted by the Texas Civil Rights Project on May 31, 2018.

"No. Bullshit. This is the mom. You have her kid. We're coming to get the kid.'"
--Jodi Goodwin, veteran Rio Grande Valley immigration attorney

Contents

Family Separation Timeline

March 3, 2017: The Trump Administration first discusses the idea of family separation at the U.S.-Mexico border, but the idea is dismissed as too controversial.

October 2017: Family separations begin in secret; according to an April 20, 2018 *New York Times* report, more than 700 children are separated between October 2017 and April 2018.

2018

April 6: Attorney General Jeff Sessions announces the nationwide zero-tolerance policy that leads to mass family separations.

April 11: Department of Homeland Security Secretary Kirstjen Nielsen testifies to Congress that no family separation policy exists.

Late May: Customs and Border Protection officials begin systematically turning away asylum seekers at ports of entry across the U.S.-Mexico border.

June 11: Sessions reverses a Board of Immigration Appeals ruling in an effort to make gang violence and domestic abuse no longer criteria for asylum.

June 14: Sessions defends the family separation policy by citing the Bible.

June 15: For the first time the Department of Homeland Security says how many children have been separated from their parents: 1,995 since April 19.

June 17: On Father's Day, a congressional delegation tours the Ursula Central Processing Center in McAllen and the Casa Padre children's shelter in Brownsville. Photos are released showing children and parents in cages under Mylar "foil" blankets.

June 18: *ProPublica* publishes a recording of children crying and calling out for their mothers inside a detention center.

June 20: President Donald Trump signs an executive order ending family separation; no provision is made for reuniting families already separated.

June 26: Judge Dana Sabraw orders that children under five must be reunited with their parents within 14 days, children five and older in 30 days.

June 30: Hundreds of thousands of people attend Families Belong Together marches nationwide.

July 10: At the first court deadline, 38 of 102 separated children under age five are reunited.

July 26: At the second court deadline, 43 percent of all separated families are together.

July 29: The ACLU files a lawsuit in defense of parents who were misled or coerced into signing paperwork that gave up their right to apply for asylum.

Angry Tías

August 3: The government argues in court that it is the responsibility of the ACLU, not the government, to reunite separated families; Judge Sabraw responds that it "is 100 percent the responsibility of the administration."

Daniel Blue Tyx

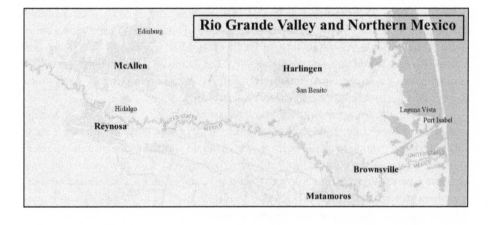

Rio Grande Valley and Northern Mexico

INTRODUCTION

One face in particular haunts me. When I met Andrea* at the Pearsall detention center, the Salvadoran mother's long, curly black hair was loosely braided into two pigtails, draped over the front of her navy government-issue sweatshirt. She must have been in her early twenties, at most. Somehow, she seemed to have safeguarded the buoyant optimism of youth, her dark eyes shining with hope. Then, bad news: A delay in her case, more paperwork to be filed. Another week until she found out when—if—she would see her toddler again. She slumped in her chair, the spark that had been present moments before drained out of her body. A week? every fiber in her being seemed to be saying. A week is an eternity.

That day was my first face-to-face encounter with the horror of family separation. A week ago, I'd been on vacation with my wife and two kids in Mexico City, blissfully tuning out the 24/7 news cycle. In spite of the anti-immigrant rhetoric now routinely spewing from our government, the city's *chilangos* had welcomed us with open arms. Every day we were stopped on busy sidewalks by total strangers saying things like, *Bienvenidos. Aquí están en su casa.* We had felt at home. My six-year-old daughter Ana cried when it was time to fly back.

The evening we arrived in McAllen, after the kids were in bed, I opened my computer and pulled up the *New York Times* website. It was Father's Day, the day a congressional delegation toured the Ursula Central Processing Center where parents and children were held in separate cages in an area called *la perrera*, or the dog pound. McAllen was the byline. I had to search on Google Maps to find out where the center was—seven miles from our house, in the "foreign-trade zone" near the border, a part of town I almost never visited. I found myself crying. *This is my actual home*, I thought.

For a few days, the initial shock left me paralyzed. As a journalist, and as a border resident, I felt a strong pull to respond. But I wasn't even sure where to begin until I saw a Facebook video posted by John Garland, an old friend from McAllen who is now a Mennonite pastor in San Antonio. He'd already spent extensive time at the border documenting family separation for his congregation and the wider faith community. "It's worse than anyone could possibly think," he said. "People need to know."

He invited me to go with him to Nuevo Laredo the following day, where he was meeting with pastors organizing emergency housing for refugees turned away at the international bridge. He also arranged for me to shadow an immigration attorney—her office was housed in his church—the day after that at a detention center halfway between Laredo and San Antonio. In Nuevo Laredo, one of the most violent cities in North America, I saw and heard about the dangers that refugees faced. At La Voz del Cielo evangelical church, an armored tank-like vehicle patrolled the street, while the middle-aged *pastora* told us about the armed men who'd stormed the shelter, which doubled as the church's sanctuary. Then, the next morning, I witnessed what refugee families faced on the U.S. side of the border.

For the hourlong trip to the detention center, I rode in the backseat of a Subaru belonging to Sara Ramey, the 35-year-old director of the nonprofit Migrant Center for Human Rights. Joining her in the front was a retired patent attorney, while next to me was an intern from Brownsville who had just finished her first year of law school and had previously worked at Casa Padre, the infamous Walmart-turned-children's-detention-center. Intensely focused, with a rapid-fire diction and encyclopedic knowledge of the law, Ramey cut back and forth between a mock-hearing with the intern—she would be appearing in court alone for the first time—and an asylum-law crash course for the patent attorney. "Do you speak Spanish?" Ramey asked me during a brief lull. *Sí*, I murmured. "Okay," she said, "you're going to be my assistant." As I was about to find out, the entire system was so overwhelmed that every bit of extra help counted.

The detention center was behind a Holiday Inn Express on the I-35 frontage road, surrounded by a chain-link fence topped with razor wire. Four flags flew at the entrance, those of the United States, Texas, Department of Homeland Security, and GEO Group, the private prison conglomerate. The company logo had a map of the world inscribed inside the letter O. Inside, we stuffed our cell phones and wallets into a locker and passed through the metal detector into a windowless lobby. To one side, I noticed an open door next to a long, narrow, rectangular room lined with stools and labeled "non-contact visitation room." There was a play table like the one at my kids' pediatrician's office next to a Coke machine.

Ramey entered a passcode into a heavy security door, and we walked down a hallway and into a courtroom. Thirteen men in navy uniforms—except for two who were inexplicably in red—sat in wooden pews, watching us. Ramey set out cardboard boxes full of documents on a pair of wooden tables, while a guard in a tan GEO cap hushed the asylum seekers, although no one seemed to be speaking above a whisper. "This is a courtroom," he admonished. Not seeing any judge, I turned to Ramey in confusion. Court wouldn't actually begin for another two hours, she said, but this was the only space available to meet with clients. Anyway, we wouldn't have to wait for each detainee to be called out individually—a process that was often delayed. "If we had more attorneys, if we had more time, we wouldn't have to do so much at once," Ramey explained.

She handed me a box full of intake forms and a yellow legal pad and explained my job. On the forms, I was to record names, alien numbers, and dates of birth, as well as information about income and savings. (One father I later interviewed had $.06 in his commissary account; a mother reported an income of one dollar a week working in the laundry room.) If there was time, I could take additional notes. I jotted down a list of questions: When did you come? How did you come? Why did you come? Were you separated from your children? How were you separated?

"Where are the women?" I overheard Ramey ask one of the guards. The guard mumbled something about a headcount earlier and walked out the door. An hour or so later, I looked up to find three women waiting in the front pew. I'd finished the intake with the men, so I listened in as Ramey delivered the bad news to the young Salvadoran woman in pigtails. I turned a page on my pad and prepared to write down everything I could.

I wasn't an immigration reporter. To the contrary, ever since I'd left a steady job as a community college professor to begin work as a freelance magazine writer five years ago, I had mostly avoided pitching stories on that beat. I told myself—not unreasonably—that this was because there were already plenty of other writers doing those stories, with more resources than I could hope to muster. But also, I think now, there was another reason. Although I grew up in the Midwest, I've lived in McAllen for fifteen years, the longest I've ever been in one place. McAllen is home, which may explain why I tried for so long to evade the dim realization that our community's economic, political, and social life is inextricably tied up with the detention of thousands of people every day who've come to our country for no other reason than to seek a better life—or to not be killed, or not have their children killed.

The majority of asylum seekers came from Honduras, Guatemala, and El Salvador, where heavily armed gangs control entire neighborhoods and swaths of territory. The roots of this violence can be traced to American military intervention in the region, when the Reagan administration supported repressive authoritarian regimes in Guatemala and El Salvador in civil wars that killed as many as 300,000 people. While there was no large-scale civil war in Honduras, the country served as the staging ground for paramilitary Contras fighting in Nicaragua, and the CIA sponsored a military battalion responsible for the disappearance of hundreds of students, human rights leaders, and members of the political opposition.

In the aftermath of these conflicts, a surfeit of militarized and often unemployed young men provided a breeding ground for the growth of organized crime, as did stepped-up deportations of criminals from the United States. By 2016, El Salvador had the highest murder rate in the world, with Honduras second, and Guatemala tenth. Some 95 percent of crimes go unpunished in the Northern Triangle, creating a culture of impunity that is especially dangerous for victims of domestic violence, which is why, in recent years, women and children have made up an ever-greater proportion of asylum seekers. After the most arduous journeys—by bus, on top of trains, in semi-trailers without ventilation, on foot—these asylum seekers finally arrived at their harbor of safety, only to have the very government they were counting on to protect them take their children away.

Back at home, I felt a sense of urgency to respond, although at first I wasn't sure how. I began by traveling, alone, to the places where the crisis was unfolding. Often, I felt foolish for even going. I went to the Ursula Central Processing Center, also known as *la hielera*, or the icebox, on account of the frigid temperatures inside that many detainees described as a form of torture. But what was I going to do except stare from outside the gate, trying to catch a glimpse of the white buses carrying parents and children, separately, that lined up hundreds of yards away, deliberately shielded from view? I had a similar experience on multiple days at the federal courthouse, where even though the proceedings were ostensibly open to the public, the guard kept turning me away because, he said, every seat in the room was already occupied by defendants.

But at the midpoint of the McAllen-Hidalgo International Bridge, where dozens of asylum seekers slept on cardboard boxes and subsisted on ham sandwiches delivered by volunteers, the crisis was in plain view. Mothers, with little to protect them from the elements, waited with toddlers, even babies. They were marooned there, stopped from going to the American side by three armed Customs and Border Protection officers, and fearful of even using the bathroom on the Mexican side, where migrants had been kidnapped for ransom from the foot of the bridge. On most summer days in the Rio Grande Valley, the families had to endure triple-digit heat, but the week I started going to the bridge it rained nonstop, a deluge that would eventually lead to a state of emergency being declared for the entire county. Everything, and everyone, was soaked; all the kids had coughs.

The bridge was where I first encountered the Angry Tías and Abuelas—or just the Tías, or aunts, for short—a group of ordinary local women who were handing out backpacks full of food, water, menstrual pads, toothbrushes, toothpaste, crayons, coloring books, even toy cars and stuffed animals, to waiting families. It was the worst of America, and it was the best of America, all condensed into one narrow stretch of suspended sidewalk that wasn't technically America at all.

The volunteers I met told me about other volunteers, who told me about other volunteers, and on it went. Across the Rio Grande Valley, from McAllen to Brownsville, more people started showing up at bridges, courthouses, detention centers, shelters, and bus stations. They wrote down the names of separated parents and their children at the federal courthouses. They organized protests. They fed and clothed asylum seekers at the bridges, and, later, at the bus stations where Immigration and Customs Enforcement (ICE) dropped off parents, often with no ticket and no money. They filled in the gaps left by a government that abnegated responsibility for the well-being of families that had fled the worst violence imaginable.

As I continued my reporting, I also met lawyers and other professional advocates and agitators who, like Sara Ramey, had dedicated their lives to working on behalf of refugees. Over time, I came to think of these dedicated professionals as Angry Tías, too. Equipped with infinitesimally small resources in comparison to the huge government bureaucracies they were fighting, they relied on personal conviction, audacity, and seemingly boundless empathy to accomplish what sometimes seemed impossible even to them, whether that meant creating a database of every separated parent and their children in government custody without the government's help, or reuniting a child with her mother in a matter of hours when the government insisted it would take weeks.

The Angry Tías of the Rio Grande Valley were—are—doing the work of democracy, in a country that at times seems to have forgotten the meaning of the word.

In this book, I have, in many cases, used interviews with activists to reconstruct scenes that occurred over the course of the summer, in an effort to tell the story of family separation through the eyes of those who observed its traumatic consequences firsthand. As much as possible, I have tried to narrate these events in chronological order. The events of the summer were often confusing, and the news reporting at times contradictory; for me, as a writer, the act of ordering these events vastly improved my understanding of what happened. I hope readers will find it the same. In other places, I've written directly about places and events that I was there to witness; here again, I did my best to fit these scenes into the chronology, but they are narrated from my own perspective.

My hope is that, in sharing these stories of border resistance, I can draw attention to a crucial, life-or-death effort that is still ongoing. At the time of this writing, hundreds of children—possibly thousands, since the government now says it doesn't have exact figures—remain separated from their parents, even as the focus of the national media has shifted elsewhere. Most if not all of these children are in imminent danger of being permanent orphans. Meanwhile, the Trump administration, apparently undeterred by the political and moral catastrophe of the crisis, continues to implement new and draconian policies, including the indefinite detention of families and children in tent cities, the assertion of its right to deny asylum seekers the opportunity to make their case before a judge, the dispatch of U.S. troops to the border to guard against the contrived threat of migrant caravans, and most dramatic of all the firing of tear gas into crowds of families and children.

Like so many geopolitical tragedies, this promises to get worse before it gets better. As 2018 came to an end, the administration's refusal to honor the right of families to seek asylum at legal ports of entry, and its lack of preparation for the inevitable consequences, led to some of the worst tragedies imaginable. On December 8, 7-year-old Jakelin Caal Maquin of Guatemala died after 11 hours in Border Patrol custody in an isolated part of New Mexico. Then, on Christmas Day, 8-year-old Felipe Gómez Alonzo, also of Guatemala, died at a hospital in the same state after days of being shuttled from one Border Patrol station to another without adequate medical care. In both cases, Border Patrol agents were ill-trained to identify the symptoms of severe illness in children whose families should never have been compelled to make the dangerous trek across the desert in the first place.

The deaths of Jakelin and Felipe could have been prevented if only a policy of ineffective deterrence were replaced by one emphasizing compassion, respect for human rights and the timely and fair processing of asylum claims. In the meantime, *la lucha continúa*—and so does the work of the Angry Tías fighting against callous cruelty here on the border.

SEPARATION

THE COURTHOUSE HAS GONE NUTS

In April, Selma Yznaga, a counseling professor at the University of Texas-Rio Grande Valley, got a call at home from one of her students, who was at work at the federal courthouse in Brownsville. "Dr. Y," the student began, "the courthouse has gone nuts. There are people screaming, people wailing. There are tons of people in here. They're shackled. What's happening?'"

In retrospect, the answer is clear. On April 6, Attorney General Jeff Sessions had first announced the Trump administration's "zero-tolerance" policy, which dictated that all adults crossing the border outside of ports of entry would be prosecuted and detained indefinitely, even if they were seeking asylum because they feared for their lives in their home countries. Asylum seekers, wearing the same clothes they had on when they crossed the Rio Grande, were led into court with shackles at their ankles, wrists, and waists. When the judge asked them to swear to tell the truth, they could only lift their hands a few inches. Some of them were parents who had been separated from their children.

For more than a decade, Yznaga had worked as a consultant for the Young Center, an organization that pairs child asylum seekers—some of whom don't have a lawyer—with mentors from the community. She was about as knowledgeable a non-lawyer as you could find when it came to asylum policy, but she didn't have any idea what to tell her student. Before zero-tolerance, only two or three misdemeanor illegal entry cases were prosecuted a week at the Brownsville courthouse. Typically, they were Mexican citizens who would be dropped off at the bridge later that afternoon. The idea of mass trials for asylum seekers from Central America seemed far-fetched, given that the border's court system was already stressed to the breaking point. Even the Department of Justice press release announcing zero-tolerance a few days earlier had contained the seemingly important caveat that prosecutions would occur "to the extent practicable." "At first, it was just unbelievable," Yznaga recalled, when I met her later in the summer at her house on a palm-lined street in central Brownsville, 60 miles east of McAllen. "I was like, 'No, that can't be happening, because that doesn't happen in the United States."

Further confusing matters was the fact that very little had changed at the border itself. The overall number of border apprehensions in the first part of 2018 was at a near-record low. Meanwhile, the number of asylum seekers had seen a slight uptick but was still average in comparison to the rest of the decade, and much lower than in 2014, when refugees, many of them unaccompanied minors, first began arriving from Central America in large numbers. By any objective measure, zero-tolerance was a solution in search of a problem. Family separation, in turn, was a manufactured crisis.

Unsure what to say or do, Yznaga called the American Civil Liberties Union, which had recently opened a regional office in Brownsville. On the other end of the line was Mike Seifert, a mild-mannered but incisive former priest who had served the parish of Cameron Park—the Rio Grande Valley's largest and most impoverished *colonia*, or unincorporated community lacking basic services—for twelve years before getting married and jumping into a second career as a community organizer. Seifert's initial reaction confirmed what Yznaga was already thinking. "We need to get to the courthouse," he said.

What Seifert had in mind wasn't totally new. It was no coincidence that the ACLU's Brownsville office had opened soon after Trump's inauguration. Given the dehumanizing rhetoric of "animals" and "bad *hombres*" of election season, Seifert had been strategizing in preparation for worst-case scenarios ever since. One idea he kept coming back to was a "court watch" program, in which ordinary citizens would attend court every day, serving as a kind of early-alert system that would identify abuses potentially weeks or months before they became widely known.

After the phone call from Yznaga, Seifert and his officemate, fellow organizer Christina Patiño Houle from a coalition of nonprofits called the Equal Voice Network, sprang into action. They recruited volunteers, created an observation form, and figured out how to use an online scheduling tool. But when the first court watchers showed up to court, the bailiff told them they couldn't go in because there wasn't room. "That only stoked everybody," Seifert told me when I visited him at the ACLU office on the second-floor of a private law firm in suburban Brownsville. Those turned away spread the word to friends and relatives, who, incensed, signed up as well. Eventually, there were 75 volunteers; after much tense back and forth, the ACLU was able to persuade the judges to let them in.

The court watchers arrived an hour early and sat down—or stood, if there was no room—at the back of the court, in time to see the defendants led in to the courtroom. When the hearing began, they spoke one after another in quick succession. *Culpable. Culpable. Culpable. Culpable.* The most important part of the hearing for the court watchers was the end, when the judge habitually asked if the defendants had anything else they wanted to say. Some days, no one spoke up at all.

But if one person did muster the courage, it could open up the floodgates. They would ask where their daughters and sons were, and when they would see them again. The court watchers, who always worked in pairs—both to be more accurate, and so that no one would have to face the often emotional experience alone—scribbled furiously, trying to keep up. Later, the information they gathered was passed on to the ACLU, which would follow up, if possible, to coordinate medical care, legal service, and phone calls.

The efforts were frustratingly piecemeal. The court watchers couldn't ask people to slow down or speak more clearly; in their capacity as observers, they weren't allowed to say anything at all. They only got information from those who spoke up. Who knew how many other dire situations went unrecorded altogether?

Still, it's significant that some of the first people to respond to family separation were ordinary residents of the Rio Grande Valley, many of whom had never before set foot in a courtroom, who showed up every day for both sessions, in the morning and in the afternoon. By early May, before most Americans had any idea what was happening at the border, the mass prosecutions were no longer happening behind closed doors. The court watchers shared their eyewitness accounts with other community members, on social media, and with the press. The names of separated parents and their children were passed onto the ACLU, who could work to arrange pro bono lawyers and, eventually, to facilitate phone conversations between the separated families.

On occasion, the presence of the court watchers also made a tangible difference in the outcome of the proceedings. The first day that Seifert, Patiño Houle, and another volunteer attended court, a Guatemalan man was being prosecuted who clearly didn't speak Spanish, only an indigenous language. Glancing nervously at the observers, the public defender asked that her client's prosecution be deferred, since there was no translator. The judge ultimately agreed. "I think that because there were three people in the back of the courtroom taking notes who were unidentified, it added a level of concern and increased awareness for what was the right thing to do," Patiño Houle told me.

The greatest impact, though, was perhaps on the volunteers themselves. They would go on to organize other groups responding to the family separation crisis across the Rio Grande Valley, including the Angry Tías and Abuelas. "It's the experience of being in the room," the ex-priest Seifert told me. "It's the stench, it's the desperation, it's the craziness. You see all those people packed in there, and then you recognize them. It's one thing to read about it, or hear about it in the news, but when you're standing in the room, you see that these people—the innocent—look a lot like my family."

Daniel Blue Tyx

WHERE IS HE? WHERE IS SHE?

On the other end of the Rio Grande Valley, in McAllen, attorney Efrén Olivares got a call from federal defender Azalea Alemán-Bendiks, who works at the McAllen courthouse. It was the Wednesday before Memorial Day, and Olivares was looking forward to a long weekend without talking about work with his wife and his 18-month-old son. But those plans changed as soon as Alemán-Bendiks began to describe what she was seeing.

For weeks, her team of public defenders had been charged with representing as many as 150 asylum seekers per day who were prosecuted under zero-tolerance for the misdemeanor crime of "illegal entry," typically punishable by a $10 fine and a sentence of time served. Now, as in Brownsville, those asylum seekers had begun speaking out at the end of court, telling the judge that they had been separated from their children at *la hielera.* "I was traveling with my son," they would say. "I was traveling with my daughter." "Where is he?" "Where is she?"

No one had an answer. The judge, visibly frustrated, had no idea. He asked the federal prosecutor, who said that Border Patrol would know. Border Patrol could only say that the Office of Refugee Resettlement, an arm of the Health and Human Services department, had taken custody of the children. But ORR had hundreds of shelters all across the country, none of which was set up to deal with separated children; they were supposed to be for unaccompanied minors—typically, teenagers who had traveled by themselves, or with a smuggler. Previously, under guidelines established during the Obama administration, parents traveling with children had been released to stay with family or friends already in the United States while their cases were heard. Now, under the auspices of zero-tolerance, even asylum-seeker parents were being prosecuted. Their children, some as young as infants, were being taken away before they left for court.

Alemán-Bendiks had gotten Olivares's number from a former colleague at the public defender's office, who now worked for the Texas Civil Rights Project, a public-interest legal nonprofit, in Houston. That colleague had connected her with Olivares, the sole lawyer at the TCRP office in the small city of Alamo, just east of McAllen. "Is there something you all can do?" Alemán-Bendiks asked.

5

Olivares, a youthful-looking 35-year-old with a gravel-lined baritone voice and a perpetual three-day beard, asked Alemán-Bendiks if she could write an affidavit to document what was happening. She checked with her supervisor and called backed 15 minutes later. "I can't do that because I would be a witness," she told him, conveying the instructions she'd been given. "But what I can do is let you come and interview our clients."

"I'll be there tomorrow morning," Olivares answered.

As a student at Yale Law School, Olivares had envisioned a globetrotting career in international human rights law. For a year after graduation, he had interned in Washington, DC, at the Inter-American Commission on Human Rights, an international tribunal that hears cases involving human rights violations by members of the Organization of American States. Life, though, had led him in different directions. While in DC, Olivares's father, who had brought his family to the Rio Grande Valley from Monterrey, Mexico, when he was 13, passed away unexpectedly. To be closer to his mother in the RGV, Olivares had taken a job at a private law firm in Houston. Four years later, he'd moved to McAllen for a job at the tiny nonprofit office where he focused on discrimination cases that, in a community that was more than 90 percent Latino, often involved citizenship status.

Olivares wasn't an immigration attorney; he knew only the basics of asylum law. Still, from his year at the Inter-American Commission, he was pretty clear on one thing: Even if the family separations Alemán-Bendiks was describing were permissible under U.S. criminal and civil law—he didn't know enough to be certain either way—they almost certainly represented a violation of international law.

The following morning, Olivares arrived with Georgina Guzman, the office's paralegal, at the McAllen federal courthouse at 7:30 a.m. The defendants were led in at eight, leaving 45 minutes for the duo to interview all 80. That first morning, five of the defendants had been separated from children, two mothers and three fathers, all from the Northern Triangle. Every one of the stories was chilling. Vilma Aracely López Juc de Coc, who was separated from her 11-year-old son, had fled Guatemala after her husband was brutally murdered. She cried through the entire interview. María Andrés de la Cruz, also from Guatemala, was separated from three children ages 11, 8, and 7. At the Border Patrol Processing Center, she was told, falsely, that she would see them right after the hearing.

Olivares had anticipated that the conversations with the defendants would be difficult. He hadn't imagined, however, that he would have to be the one to break the news that they might not see their children again, at least not right away. "I hope that's true," Olivares told the parents, when they asked if they would be reunited after court, as many of them had been told. "But I think that might not be the case. We're going to try our best so that it's soon, but it may be a few days, or a few weeks. I don't want to lie to you. I can't tell you exactly when."

Casting aside his weekend plans, Olivares worked around the clock on a petition formally known as an Emergency Request for Precautionary Measures, which was filed the following Thursday, May 31. It read in part:

> This Request challenges the systematic separation of parents from their children—without notice, information, or the opportunity to challenge the separation—and the inability for parents to communicate with their children and know their whereabouts as well as the lack of process to allow for reunification.

Originally, Olivares planned to go back to his regular caseload after the request was filed. But the initial day at the courthouse convinced him otherwise. Forty-five minutes wasn't enough time to record everyone's stories in depth, but it was enough to determine the number of separated parents, and to record their names and dates of birth, as well as those of their children. That information, he foresaw, could be vital in helping parents locate and get in contact with their children later on. The information could also be used, eventually, to help connect clients with pro bono lawyers who could take on their asylum cases. "We quickly realized that unless we were there to capture that information, these people would go into a black hole in the system, and nobody would be trying to reunite them," Olivares said.

Since the day after Memorial Day, a Texas Civil Rights Project staff member has attended every court session in McAllen. At the height of the crisis, they interviewed 34 separated parents in one day. In total, they documented the cases of 382 separated parents. "I understand that the government has provided lists," Olivares told me," but there's no way to corroborate those lists. Except for the 382 that we interviewed, it's only the government at its word."

One of the questions Olivares and the other staff members always asked was how the parents were separated from their children. The answers left him stunned. Sometimes the children were taken from the cages at *la perrera* to be transported to an ORR shelter in the middle of the night, while the parent was asleep. Sometimes they were dragged away, screaming, as the parent looked on. Sometimes, as in María's case, the separation occurred when the parent was loaded onto the bus bound for the federal courthouse. Once, a mother had her infant son taken away while she was breastfeeding. On two separate occasions, mothers were told that the officers were just taking their daughters for a bath.

Olivares told me that he felt a particular emotional connection to the fathers, perhaps because he was a new father himself. One story that particularly moved him, which he later wrote about in a *New York Times* op-ed, concerned a father who, at the moment he was separated from his seven-year-old daughter, told her that she was going to a summer camp. She left with a big smile; it reminded him of the film *Life Is Beautiful*.

Olivares endured daily reminders of what his clients must be going through. Over the summer, his son began going to daycare. On the first day, his wife received an urgent phone call from the day care, asking her to please come back. Their son was despondent, and although the staff tried everything they could think of to console and comfort him, nothing had worked. "And it was only one hour!" he told me. "It was a small reminder of what these families are going through. They haven't seen their children for weeks, some of them months. They were fleeing a country in order to protect their children, but just when they thought they'd made it, they had their child taken away."

THE BIG CORRAL

On Memorial Day, first thing in the morning, Jodi Goodwin drove through a gap in a chain-link fence topped with spiraling double rows of razor wire, and down a long, palm-lined driveway to the Port Isabel Detention Center. Known as *el corralón*, or the big corral, the prison—"that's the only thing to call it," Goodwin says—is tucked away out of view from the highway on 375 acres of land at the site of a former naval base on the banks of the Laguna Madre, next to the Rio Grande Valley's largest national wildlife refuge. Eventually, Goodwin reached the first of two guard posts. She showed her driver's license and proof of insurance before parking her car and heading inside to visit for the first time with six separated mothers.

At the end of the previous week, Goodwin had also received a call from a public defender's office, this one in Brownsville. She'd heard the same story as in McAllen. Hysterical parents pleaded to find out where their children were; judges and lawyers had no answers to give them. Unlike in McAllen, though, the judges weren't allowing outside lawyers in to interview separated parents. Goodwin was going where she knew she could find them: Port Isabel, the largest detention center in the Rio Grande Valley, with the capacity to hold 1,175 adult detainees.

Inside, Goodwin, who has practiced immigration law out of her office in Harlingen—halfway between McAllen and Brownsville—for 23 years, worked the system like she always did, bantering good-naturedly with the guards. At Port Isabel, as at other detention centers, lawyers have to ask for clients to be "called out" by a guard. Delays for all sorts of reasons—headcounts, meals, stonewalling— are routine; a good relationship with everyone from the guards to the legal secretaries to the ICE attorneys made the system work a little more efficiently. That part of the job came naturally to the gregarious Goodwin, who always remembered to ask about staff members' kids, some of whom went to school with her own children. A native of the tiny East Texas rice farming community of Old River, the blond, matronly Goodwin reminded me a bit of the former Texas governor Ann Richards, who won respect even from people she didn't agree with through a combination of natural warmth and blunt straight talk—often punctuated by a healthy dose of four-letter words.

Since zero-tolerance, even Goodwin had found the waiting much worse than usual. Asking around, she was told that the designated attorney rooms were not currently "available," since they had been taken over by public health staff. When she grilled the nurses, none of whom she'd ever seen before, all she was able to learn was that they were on a weeklong tour. What for? They were vague: A few DNA tests and other, unspecified, duties for "the mission."

An hour after she arrived, once a room was finally located, the first mother arrived. Goodwin did preliminary intake, and then began to fill her in on the next step in the process: a one-hour "credible-fear" interview with an asylum officer, which would determine if her case went forward to be heard by an immigration judge, or if she would be placed in deportation proceedings. Historically, 70 percent of asylum seekers at Port Isabel passed the credible-fear stage; if she failed, she still had the option to appeal to a judge.

The woman listened intently, waiting until Goodwin was finished to ask the two questions that clearly had been on her mind the entire time. First, when would she see her daughter again? And second, could Goodwin talk to the other women in her pod who were in the same situation?

At Port Isabel, "pod" is the name given each dormitory, a setup that has been compared to an aquarium. Detainees are housed in a circular configuration around a glassed-in guard booth, from where the guard cannot only see everything—including the partitionless shared toilet—but also control everything from the lights to the TV stations. It felt dehumanizing, but the pods also transformed over time into a sort of community. With no access to the Internet, and a limited ability to make phone calls—they cost money, which almost no one had—the women turned to the only people they felt they could trust for help: each other. "How many mothers have been separated from their children in your pod?" Goodwin asked.

"Seventy," the woman answered. *Shit*, Goodwin thought, beginning to fathom for the first time the scale of the crisis. When the second mother was called in, the same scene unfolded. She was in a different pod. The same with the third mother. In the end, the six mothers Goodwin interviewed were housed in five different pods. Each told the same story. Goodwin quickly did the math in her head: 350 moms.

Back at her office later that night, Goodwin shared her findings with her law partner, Sarah Vidal. "Sarah, there's no way we can do this," she said. "There are simply not enough hours in the day."

At 9:50 on Tuesday night, Goodwin was still at her office working when she heard her phone ring. Glancing down, she saw that it was a lawyer friend in D.C. with whom she frequently talked shop. She picked up, but they'd just gotten past hello when her friend put someone else on the line. It was Ali Rahnama, a civil rights attorney. "Hi," he said, "I'm bringing 10 lawyers to help you with the family separation crisis."

"Who are you?" Goodwin replied.

Rahnama was part of a group of D.C.-area lawyers that had first organized to respond at the airports during the chaotic first days of the Trump administration's Muslim ban. Since then, they had fashioned themselves into a sort of legal SWAT team, prepared to respond at a moment's notice to the Trump administration's latest outrage. "It just fell in our lap," Goodwin told me later, when we met at a conference table in her nondescript private law office on Harlingen's main strip. "I hadn't even thought far enough ahead to figure out, 'How can I recruit people to help us?'"

As promised, the lawyers arrived on Wednesday night, less than 24 hours later. In the meantime, Goodwin, who had already decided to put off most of her regular caseload for the rest of the summer, formulated a plan. First, the lawyers would take on the massive challenge of intake for however many hundreds of separated parents were at the detention center. Next, they would use that information to locate their children, and establish a connection by phone. It could also be shared with RAICES, the San Antonio nonprofit that was coordinating a master list of all separated parents nationwide, including those flagged by the Texas Civil Rights Project and court watchers. Ultimately, that list would be shared with ICE, because, as Goodwin explained, "ICE didn't know who they had. They had no plan, no recordkeeping about which parents belonged to which kids."

Then, the lawyers could move ahead with parents' asylum cases. Initially, that meant prepping for the credible-fear interviews. Most asylum seekers had little knowledge of the legal system, or even what the credible-fear interview was or why it was important. The hour or so Goodwin typically spent with new clients explaining the process was vitally important to the ultimate success of their cases. But in the early days of family separation, she'd found that none of the parents wanted to talk about their cases, no matter how much she emphasized that it held the key to their liberty. "They were not concerned with that," she told me. "They wanted to know where their kids were. It was a lot of consoling of people who were going through really traumatic situations."

Meanwhile, ICE, eager to open up more beds at the detention center as quickly as possible, rushed to get through as many interviews as they could. Many asylum seekers had their interview before they ever met with a lawyer. Sometimes they would spend the entire session just trying to learn more information about their child instead of answering the officer's questions.

Goodwin's experience with the credible-fear interviews, and the situation at Port Isabel more generally, was echoed in an August complaint filed with DHS by the American Immigration Lawyers Association that drew on sworn affidavits from 13 parents. One Honduran woman, named in the complaint as D.P., who had been separated from her 9-year-old daughter, described her interview in this way:

> I could not control my emotions, I was only thinking about my daughter. I did not even realize when the officer asked me different questions related to my asylum case. The asylum officer asked me why I left, and I said because I was threatened and beaten, and that is why I left. And when the asylum officer in response required [me] to provide more details, I started to cry. Because I cried a lot, the asylum officer raised his voice again. Instead of providing more details, I started asking where my child was. In response, he said that if I wanted to know where my daughter was, he recommended me to watch the news. I told him I did not have any access to the news. And that is how the interview was ended.

Later, after D.P. was informed of a negative credible fear decision, she was called to an interview with an ICE officer the other mothers in her pod called "the deporter." He insisted that she sign deportation papers—parents were often promised that they would be reunited with their children if they signed, and many did—and yelled at her when she refused. "Fine," he told her, "stay in detention for a year waiting for your daughter."

Finally, after 10 days of the team working from early morning until they were kicked out of Port Isabel at 9:15 p.m., Goodwin began to feel that the tide was turning. They'd figured out how to successfully navigate ICE's labyrinthine bureaucracy so that parents could begin speaking to their children on the phone, making it easier to prep their cases. Although the first wave of rapid-response lawyers had to go home after two weeks, reinforcements were on the way in the form of lawyers from Kids in Need of Defense, another legal advocacy group. Though she hesitated to even say it out loud, Goodwin began to feel quietly confident that they'd reached the mountaintop and could now see over to the other side.

Then, another policy reversal from the Trump administration jeopardized all the thousands of hours of legal work that Goodwin's team had put in so far. Under the Refugee Act of 1980, people who arrive to the United States are eligible for asylum if they fear being killed or harmed in their home countries based on one of five criteria—race, religion, nationality, political opinion, or membership in a particular social group. The last category has long been understood to include gender, and many women have won asylum based on evidence of domestic violence, often ignored or even condoned by corrupt and ineffectual law enforcement at home.

But on June 11, Attorney General Sessions issued a ruling that shocked even veteran lawyers like Goodwin. Drawing on an arcane provision of the law that permitted the Attorney General to intervene in immigration case appeals, Sessions reversed an appeals court decision in a case called *Matter of A-B-* in which a Guatemalan woman was granted asylum because she feared for her life after being repeatedly beaten by her husband. The rationale for the decision was remarkably broad: People fleeing "private criminal activity," even that which was ignored by law enforcement, should not be eligible for asylum. According to Sessions, that ruled out both domestic abuse and gang violence.

Almost overnight, the credible-fear passage rate at Port Isabel, which had previously been about 70 percent, plummeted. "Nobody was passing," Goodwin told me. "Nobody. Just the occasional two or three people." The volunteer lawyers rushed to document who had passed or failed the interview, and to file appeals for the vast majority who had failed. The process, though, was complicated by the fact that the government wouldn't release the results of the interviews to lawyers, only to the clients themselves, and then only by means of vaguely worded form letters. Just to find out who needed to file an appeal, Goodwin's team had to call out all 400 or so separated parents, one at a time, even though ICE was still saying that the attorney rooms were all booked. Even then, it was next to impossible to tell why the client had failed and on what grounds they might be able to mount a challenge.

Immediately, Goodwin launched a massive new effort, calling not just on the out-of-town lawyers, but also dozens of friends and colleagues from the Rio Grande Valley legal community, who flooded Port Isabel over the course of a weekend in a last-ditch effort to speak with every parent. If they filed an appeal, there was still hope. The Sessions ruling contradicted the precedents of numerous other cases; the legal tangle would only be unknotted after months—or years—in court. But for parents the lawyers weren't able to reach in time, it would already be too late. They would be deported without their children. In some cases, it had already happened.

A REFUGEE CAMP AT THE BRIDGE

By May 31, nearly 2,000 children had been separated from their parents at the border, although that figure wasn't published until June 15, right before Father's Day. As details slowly leaked out and pressure began to build to end the family separation policy, the Trump administration, led by Department of Homeland Security Secretary Kirstjen Nielsen—who initially denied that family separation was a policy at all—began trotting out a new line of defense: Asylum seekers who didn't want to be prosecuted and separated from their children should apply for asylum "legally" at ports of entry. In other words, they should show up at the bridge instead of crossing the river.

But even as Nielsen argued for a "right way" to apply for asylum, officials at the bridges all along the U.S.-Mexico border began turning asylum seekers away, claiming that the offices where they were processed were "too full." It was a Catch-22. Many asylum seekers, not knowing when, if ever, they would be allowed to apply at the bridge, crossed the river and turned themselves into Border Patrol on the other side. Others began sleeping just outside the door-size metal turnstiles that separated the bridges and the air-conditioned Customs and Border Patrol offices—which certainly didn't look full—in the hope that, eventually, officials would let them through. Such was the situation when veteran civil rights attorney Jennifer Harbury first arrived at the McAllen-Hidalgo International Bridge at the beginning of June.

Harbury is perhaps most famous for leaking the *ProPublica* tape of children inside a detention center crying and calling out to their parents. Described to me by one local activist as "a kind of Michelangelo of the Rio Grande Valley" for her pioneering legal advocacy, she has worked on behalf of refugees at the border for decades. Near the beginning of the Trump administration, Harbury began documenting sporadic cases of asylum seekers turned away at the bridge, which put her into frequent contact with a group of Catholic sisters who ran the *Casa del Migrante* shelter in the sprawling, violent border metropolis of Reynosa. That practice appeared to have stopped after the American Immigration Council filed a class-action lawsuit in California. But then, in late May, Harbury received an urgent call from the sisters. This time, they told her, not just a few migrants were being turned away under varying pretexts. It was *everyone*, for no reason at all.

Harbury rushed to the bridge to see for herself. Then she pulled out her phone. The first person she called was Kimi Jackson, the director of ProBAR—a nonprofit that offers legal representation to asylum seekers at Port Isabel—who in turn texted back and forth with Joyce Hamilton, a retired adult literacy educator who had helped organize a Rio Grande Valley Women's March after Trump's election. Through text messages and social media, the three women quickly organized a caravan that traveled to the bridge with coolers full of water and sandwiches. They arrived to find 40 people camped out, sleeping on cardboard boxes and using the bathroom at the duty-free shop that sold discounted perfume, liquor, and cigarettes, until it closed for the night. "They'd been camped out for five days," Hamilton remembers, "and there were babies and small children. It really did look like a refugee camp on the bridge."

That night, Jackson posted a list of needed items on her Facebook page. It was quickly shared across the Valley. Eventually, it reached Nayelly Barrios, a 32-year-old purple-haired poet and composition instructor at the University of Texas-Rio Grande Valley. Although she'd never met Jackson, she messaged her right away. "I don't live that far from the bridge," she wrote. "I can go over and take things." She shared her plan with friends on Facebook. By the next morning, she'd received $200 in donations to her PayPal account. She and her mother spent most of the day shopping and making sandwiches. Then, in the late afternoon they headed to the bridge.

Barrios was an immigrant, having moved to the Rio Grande Valley from Reynosa with her mother when she was nine. As they distributed the supplies, they conversed in Spanish with the parents, asking where they came from, what they had experienced, and what they needed. Everyone was grateful for the food and water. But to Barrios' surprise, what they most appreciated were the flip-flops, a dollar-store purchase she'd made on a whim. Few of the migrants' shoes had survived the journey. As they waited at the bridge, the hot concrete would burn the soles of their feet under the scorching South Texas sun.

For Barrios, going to the bridge was an incredibly intense experience. Although she has been politically active since college, mainly attending protests and rallies, the work at the bridge represented a new kind of activism. "It's a whole different type of emotional experience when you're face to face with people who are so vulnerable, and there's so much going against them," she told me later, when I met her at a coffee shop near the university, where she was busy prepping her fall syllabus. "It was overwhelming at first."

Barrios intended to make just one trip. But the waiting asylum seekers she met told her about other needs such as bedding, menstrual pads, and clean underwear. She came back again the next day and talked to more people. Ten or so asylum seekers were being allowed through for processing each day, but many more were arriving to take their places. She came every day that week, sometimes twice. By Friday, the size of the original group had nearly doubled, to 70 people. The makeshift camp, pushed up against a metal fence to allow room for the thousands of other pedestrians—mainly border residents who used the bridge to get to work or visit family members on the other side—began spilling out onto the bridge itself, nearly to the middle, where a bronze plaque with a vertical line down the center demarcated the official international boundary.

Still, in spite of the triple-digit heat, the weeklong waits, and the uncertainty over what lay ahead, Barrios was surprised to find a sense of camaraderie beginning to take hold. That Friday, Barrios arrived with a load of men's basketball shorts from Goodwill. She'd noticed that almost everyone had just the clothes they wore, and most of the fathers in particular wore jeans ill-suited for the heat, and uncomfortable to sleep in. The gym shorts were a huge hit. When the last of the men, a boyish Honduran named Michael, emerged from the duty-free store restroom with his shorts, perhaps a size or more too small, exposing a good part of his skinny thighs, everybody started whistling and carrying on. "*Eh, Michael, qué bien te ves,*" they razzed, laughing good-naturedly.

For Barrios, it had been an emotionally draining week, and seeing how the bridge refugee camp had transformed into a kind of makeshift community lifted her spirits. "Even though it was such an unfortunate situation to be in," Barrios remembered, "they could still find closeness and comfort in each other. That was really nice."

When Barrios arrived at the bridge the next morning, still feeling upbeat after the rare lighthearted moment the night before, she knew right away that something was wrong. Where before there had been dozens of asylum seekers, including many babies and toddlers, now there were only leftover boxes and trash strewn across the concrete. For a moment, she stood paralyzed: Where had they all gone?

Trying not to let her mind be overtaken by fears, Barrios set out to get answers. Near the amusement-park-style turnstile where you inserted your four quarters to cross over to the Mexican side of the bridge, she found another volunteer whom she recognized from a local church group that had also been dropping off supplies. The volunteer had been there two hours earlier, when Customs and Border Protection officials abruptly began calling all of the families into the office. Once they were inside, a trio of husky, navy-uniformed officers marched to the halfway point of the international bridge, where they stationed themselves directly in front of the official bronze plaque. They were asking for travel documents, turning away asylum seekers with the same line that there was "no room." Now, though, they would have to wait on the Mexican side of the bridge.

Barrios was first astonished, then infuriated as she considered the consequences of the change in policy. "Waiting on the bridge was not comfortable, but it was still safer than waiting on the Mexican side," she told me. "There are too many risks and dangers on the Mexican side for them." She pulled out her phone and posted on Facebook that there was an emergency at the bridge.

ANGRY TÍAS AND ABUELAS

No one was as intimately acquainted with the dangers that Central American migrants faced in Reynosa as Jennifer Harbury. In 2017, one of her clients, a Guatemalan woman who was one of the earlier group of asylum seekers turned away by Customs and Border Protection before the class-action lawsuit, was kidnapped from the foot of the bridge. She eventually escaped, after a week being held for ransom in a small shed on the outskirts of the city.

Harbury had every reason to believe that such kidnappings were not an anomaly, but rather an expected outcome if migrants were stranded at the bridge. The powerful cartels that were battling for control of the city, the *Cartel del Golfo* and the *Zetas*, routinely kidnapped migrants and demanded up to $10,000 in ransom, knowing that many travelers had loved ones already in the United States who might pay at least part of that sum. Those who didn't were often killed; the remains of hundreds of Central Americans had been found in *fosas*, or mass graves, across the entire state of Tamaulipas. And asylum seekers could hardly expect to turn to local law enforcement for protection, since their complicity with organized crime was an open secret. Already, Harbury was hearing that Mexican immigration officials, apparently in cooperation with the American authorities on the other side, were conducting sweeps of the bridge, arresting or threatening Central Americans who lacked a document called a transit visa that they were supposed to have obtained on the Guatemalan border. (Few had, because the office that distributed them was reputedly monitored by gangs, who could then target their recipients.)

Receiving the news from the bridge, Jennifer Harbury called a meeting at her house for that same night, inviting everyone who'd been involved in the work to that point to discuss how to respond. The anger of the eight women who gathered there was palpable. Now, on top of family separations, which psychologists and pediatricians said would cause incalculable trauma with potentially lifelong effects on children, the United States government was also knowingly putting the very lives of families at risk. Still, anger wasn't the only thing uniting the women, but also a shared sense that, no matter how bad the situation might be, they were committed to action.

Everyone at Harbury's house knew someone else, but no one knew everybody. They came from diverging walks of life, and their personalities varied widely. Harbury and Kimi Jackson were hard-nosed lawyers who had dedicated their professional lives to working with asylum seekers. Joyce Hamilton, a strait-laced retired adult education instructor who initially struck other members as a prim "church lady" before they saw how tough she could be, was motivated by a religious conviction that both governments and individuals had a responsibility to live out the gospel admonition to welcome the stranger. Cindy Candia-Luna, an imposing and outwardly brusque ex-correctional officer who had grown up in a migrant farmworker family, was following in a family tradition; her father had been active in union organizing in Washington state. Nayelly Barrios was inspired by her feminism and progressive politics, and by her own experiences as an immigrant. Besides this initial core group, there were two Catholic sisters from San Antonio's Interfaith Welcome Coalition, who brought on-the-ground expertise from the years they had worked with refugees just released from ICE detention and dropped off at the city's Greyhound bus station. Last, Candia-Luna had also invited a tech-savvy young editor from *Neta RGV*—a progressive Latinx website that had launched in the Rio Grande Valley the day after Trump's inauguration—who had offered to help with online fundraising.

The women agreed on the need for a broader, organized response to what was happening at the bridges as well as the courthouses, detention centers, bus stations, and other locales across the Rio Grande Valley. Relying on the diverse experiences of each attendee, they began to plot strategy: Where could they make the biggest difference? Where could their voices be amplified the loudest to let the rest of the world know what was going on?

They organized a Facebook group chat that, over the course of the summer, would become the nervous system for the whole group, alerting them as conditions changed on the ground, and new challenges presented themselves. At some point during the meeting, someone commented that everyone present was either a *tía*, an *abuela*, or both. It went without saying that all the aunts and grandmothers gathered were beyond angry. When it came time to decide on a name, they realized they already had one. The Angry Tías and Abuelas of the Rio Grande Valley were born.

In the weeks that followed, the Tías, as the group became known, organized a backpack-stuffing party in the fellowship hall of Hamilton's church. They filled 150 backpacks with snacks, water, clothes, toiletries, toys, and coloring books; the supplies were purchased with funds from the online crowdfunding campaign *Neta RGV* helped set up, which raised $72,000 in the first week. Passport-carrying volunteers walked through customs on the Mexican side with the backpacks, hoping not to run into problems with corrupt or overzealous inspectors, before turning back around and distributing them to the families waiting in the middle of the bridges.

In Brownsville and its sister city of Matamoros, the Tías also partnered with a group called *Ayudándoles a Triunfar*, or Helping Them Triumph, led by Glady Cañas Aguilar, who had worked for a government-funded relief agency before setting up her own independent *Asociación Civil*, the Mexican equivalent of a nonprofit. By virtue of being a Mexican citizen living in Matamoros, Cañas Aguilar could get supplies to arriving migrants more quickly, without having to deal with customs. She also coordinated with the Mexican *Cruz Roja*, or Red Cross, to provide medical care on the bridge to travelers who were sick or injured. Aiding in the efforts at the bridge were a group of young people whom her two daughters, ages 18 and 21, helped organize via social media. They helped distribute supplies, but also just took time to play with the kids, who were often bored and irritable after so long a wait, giving the parents time to go to the restroom or make calls to family members on cell phones donated by the Tías.

Along with Cañas Aguilar in Matamoros, the family tree of Tías and Abuelas in the Rio Grande Valley continued to grow. Tías began to visit mothers at Port Isabel to offer moral and logistical support, coordinating with Jodi Goodwin and investigative reporter Debbie Nathan, who provided the alien numbers that friends and relatives needed to gain admittance. Not that it was easy: Only one person was allowed to visit at a time, and they often had to wait for hours to actually speak with a mother.

Mary Alice Carlson, a retired ESL and GED teacher, waited for more than two hours to meet with María, a Honduran mother. Eventually, she was escorted to the visitation area, where she spoke to María by telephone through a thick sheet of plate glass. That separation was hard for Carlson, who wanted to be able to reach out with a reassuring touch. Still, she found it to be a meaningful connection for both of them. "I wanted to let them know that there were people out there who really did care and were there for them as much as possible," she told me. In a subsequent meeting, Carlson was able to deposit money into María's commissary account so that she could afford to make phone calls to her daughter in North Carolina. She also began a "class through the glass," teaching María some introductory English. "She was just thrilled," Carlson reported. "It felt right to be there. I felt like these were my people—María was just like the women I worked with [in her ESL classes]."

Another Tía who would quickly assume a central, if mostly behind-the-scenes role, was Madeleine Sandefur, a former office manager who took on much of the responsibility for organizing the group's finances and scheduling. Sandefur describes herself as an "accidental activist." A native of Switzerland, she met her husband, a U.S. Airman from San Antonio, in Paris in the 1970s. I first met her at the clubhouse of the South Padre Island Golf Club, where she and her husband had retired. Not long after the move, he was diagnosed with Alzheimer's, and she was his primary caretaker.

As a way to get out of the house, and because it was a popular hobby in the Rio Grande Valley, Sandefur had taken up birdwatching. That, in turn, had led to an interest in environmental issues, which is how she met Joyce Hamilton. When she first heard about family separation, it had struck a deep chord inside her. "I grew up in a household where you respect authority no matter what," she told me over chicken salad and ginger ale, "and sometimes it's hard for me to rail about what's going on. But I feel that if you don't do anything, you're complicit, right? This is not the country that I signed up for to become a citizen."

Sandefur was the driving force between the Tías' first public action. On June 14, rallies were planned nationwide as part of the Families Belong Together campaign. Sandefur and Hamilton, wanting to participate, scoured the newspapers and social media for word about where the protest would be held locally, assuming that more established organizations would take up the cause. When the day arrived, and no one had planned anything, they took matters into their own hands. They threw together an impromptu rally outside the Brownsville federal courthouse via Facebook posts, texts, and phone calls. Fifteen people, all women, showed up. So did the newspaper and the local Fox affiliate.

At the same time the rally was taking place in Brownsville, Attorney General Sessions was speaking to a group of police officers in Fort Wayne, Indiana. One of the reporters at the courthouse, glancing at the news feed on her phone, happened to see coverage of his remarks, in which he cited a portion of the Bible, Romans 13, to justify family separation. She read the quote to the Tías, and Hamilton flew into a rage. "We almost changed the name then and there from Angry Tías and Abuelas to Angry and Rampaging Abuelas," Sandefur told me. Hamilton knew that the same passage that Sessions referenced about obedience to authority had been used to justify slavery and segregation. Then as now, it was taken out of context. If Sessions had just kept quoting the same chapter, Hamilton knew, he would have eventually gotten to: "Whatever other commandment that there may be, are summed up in this saying, 'You shall love your neighbor as yourself.'"

"I mean, it's outrageous to use the Bible as justification to rip small children and babies from their parents' arms," Hamilton told the reporters. Later, I asked Hamilton about that moment at one of the Tías' backpack stuffing parties. She told me it was a turning point. "It was our first venture into realizing that our voices were going to be heard in a lot of places, and that our actions would continue to be important."

REUNION

MAMA BEAR

Late in the evening, at a dining room table at La Posada Providencia—a shelter for released asylum seekers—Jodi Goodwin sat with Anita, a Honduran mother who had been separated from her 5-year-old son Jenri. Anita was in her twenties, with dark, attentive eyes that took in all the details of her new surroundings. Her long black hair was tied up in a bun. She'd been released on bond, but her son was still in ORR custody. Goodwin told Anita that they would go to the shelter on the following day and try to get him out, but there was no guarantee that it would work.

It was July 12. The following day would mark exactly a month to the day since Anita and Jenri had been separated at *la hielera*. A little more than a week after that, on June 20, President Trump issued an executive order that officially ended the family separation policy. But it did not address the issue of how—or if—the government would reunite the families that had already been separated.

Then, on June 26, Judge Dana Sabraw of the United States District Court for the Southern District of California ordered that the federal government reunite all separated children under the age of five by July 10, and all other children by July 26. Sabraw's ruling, coming from a judge put on the bench by President George W. Bush, was a sweeping condemnation of the family separation policy, which he described as "a chaotic circumstance of the government's own making" in violation of the due process clause of the 14th Amendment. "The unfortunate reality," Sabraw wrote, "is that under the present system, migrant children are not accounted for with the same efficiency and accuracy as property."

The Sabraw injunction meant that Anita and Jenri would be reunited, eventually, but Goodwin wasn't waiting for the government to act. In a kind of macabre mental calculus, she estimated that for every day a child—especially one as young as Jenri—was separated from his mother, it would add another year of trauma to their life. She'd been visiting Anita regularly at Port Isabel, and knew the anguish she was going through. Often, they'd both cried for much of the visit.

In Honduras, Anita and Jenri were threatened at gunpoint by gang members. Moments later, without any clear plan, just a desire to escape imminent tragedy, she grabbed a bagful of clothes and began the long journey to the United

States. At Port Isabel, she became one of the lucky few who passed the credible-fear interview after the attorney general's *Matter of A-B-*reversal. When Goodwin called ICE to arrange for bond, though, the first person she spoke with informed her that, after the Sabraw decision, ICE was no longer granting bond. Goodwin knew this wasn't true: It was either a deliberate obfuscation or the result of policy being implemented haphazardly on the ground by staff who lacked clear instruction from D.C. She persisted, asking to talk with a supervisor. Eventually, a few hours later, the bond was set.

The next step was to locate Jenri and coordinate his release. After running into several dead ends, Goodwin finally got ahold of the ORR caseworker supervising Jenri's case. The caseworker told her that ORR still hadn't finished all of the required background checks. That might take several days, or more. "No," Goodwin replied. "Bullshit. This is the mom. You have her kid. We're coming to get the kid."

She told them that they would be there to pick up Jenri the next day at 4:30, and that a film crew from *The Atlantic*, which had been shadowing Goodwin for a documentary in production, would be with them. The conversation ended without any firm commitment, although at least the caseworker hadn't said no. Meanwhile, Goodwin had managed to get the piece of information she needed most: an address. She was ecstatic when she heard that the shelter wasn't in some other state, as was often the case, but rather in the Rio Grande Valley, not that far from Port Isabel.

At the dinner table at La Posada, as the film crew captured their interactions, Goodwin went over all the possible complications that could arise when they tried to get Jenri released the following day. They could be arrested for trespassing. They might have to camp out outside the front door of the shelter with the film crew. Anita nodded. She was okay, she said, with whatever risk they would have to take. Then, she started to cry.

"Hey," Goodwin told her in Spanish, looking her in the eye, "we're going to fight. We're going to save those tears for when we get your son back. Because from here on out—there's a phrase in English, 'The Mama Bear comes out.' It's the Mama Bear. We're going to do it like the Mama Bear tomorrow."

The following morning, Goodwin and Anita drove to the shelter. As Goodwin expected, the staff was furious that she'd followed through on her threat to bring the media with her. But it worked. The film crew had to wait outside, but Goodwin and Anita were allowed to wait in the lobby. Eventually, a staff member brought Jenri, carrying a new Marvel superheroes backpack and wearing a new pair of black-and-white tennis shoes.

He didn't run to his mother. Instead, he sat down on a metal folding chair, as the staff, as if reciting from a prepared script, chattered cheerfully. "Jenri, tell them how much fun you had here. Didn't you have a dinosaur toy in your room? Oh, count to ten for your mom. You learned to count while you were here!"

Anita ran to Jenri and knelt down in front of the chair to embrace him. Tears streamed from her eyes. "*Perdóname,*" she pleaded. Forgive me. "*Perdóname. Perdóname. Pérdoname.*"

Over the course of the summer, Goodwin personally reunited 11 children with their mothers. With only one exception—that of a much older teenager who surprised his mom by sitting down in her lap—she told me that every reunification went almost exactly the same way. The children had a flat affect, their faces expressionless, devoid of emotion. It sometimes took minutes to just convince the child who the mother really was. It took even more time before they were receptive to a touch.

In later reunifications, drawing on her experience with Anita and other mothers, Goodwin started trying to teach the moms how to handle the reunions. She would explain that her son or daughter would probably be withdrawn at first, and that they might be overwhelmed by a rush to embrace them, especially since in ORR custody both staff and other children were strictly prohibited from touching them. She would role-play the reunification with them beforehand, at La Posada, showing the mothers how to incrementally approach their child, so that the child wouldn't just go stiff. Often, the mothers would cry during the practice. "I'm not here to make you cry," she would tell them. "I want you to be prepared for what's going to happen, because I've seen it too much."

The same day that Anita and Jenri were reunited, Madeleine Sandefur of the Angry Tías drove to the Port Isabel Detention Center to pick up María, another of Goodwin's clients, and the mother that Tía Mary Alice Carlson had been teaching English. She was also from Honduras, and had shared a pod with Anita, where the two women became close. Like Anita, she was being released on bond. She was hoping to soon be reunited with her 11 year-old-son Abisai, who was already in New Orleans with his father, María's husband, whom she hadn't seen in years.

Goodwin had come to rely on the Tías to do many of the things that her bare-bones staff simply didn't have time to do; they were stretched so thin that a high school intern had taken over the mammoth task of communicating with prospective volunteers who were flooding an outdated website with offers to help. The Tías called shelters in cities across the country—Houston, Dallas, Seattle—to arrange housing for mothers traveling from Port Isabel to be reunited with their children, and coordinated airline and bus tickets for them to get there. Goodwin knew that she could count on the Tías if she needed something, even if it was in the middle of the night. "I don't know how they have the stamina that they have, to be quite honest," she told me. "They'll be out at the bridges, and then they're at the bus station, and then they're coordinating a rally. I love them. When I grow up, I want to be like them."

Sandefur usually worked behind the scenes because of her husband's Alzheimer's. But the South Padre Island Golf Club, where she lived, was only a short drive away from the detention center. When the call went out over Facebook Messenger, looking for someone to pick up María, she'd called the home health-care aide to care for her husband, and offered to drive her to La Posada.

Sandefur had been to the detention center once before, to visit with one of the mothers. She'd gone with a group, and had ended up waiting outside because they were told only one person could go in; the three women had picked the person who spoke the most Spanish. This time, she went alone. ICE didn't give a precise time when parents would be released, just a general window between 6:00 and 9:00 p.m. Reading materials and cell phones weren't allowed. She was prepared for a long wait, but after she gave the one of the guards María's name and alien number, and confirmed that she was indeed on the list of detainees scheduled to be released, he'd given her a heads up that she could wait in her car. "They'll be a little white minivan pulling up to the curb," he told her. "She'll probably be in that minivan."

At last, around 9 p.m., after three hours of waiting, the minivan arrived. María, who was in her forties, with deeply creased crow's feet on either side of her eyes, climbed into the front seat of Sandefur's small SUV. On the drive over to La Posada, they did their best to communicate, between Sandefur's limited Spanish and María's equally limited English. Sandefur told her how much she disagreed with what the government was doing. "That was an experience I'll never forget," María responded, referring to the time in the detention center. Sandefur told me that she could see the suffering in her eyes.

When she arrived at La Posada, María quickly found Anita. They embraced. Then, María caught sight of Jenri. Her entire face was illuminated, and tears began streaming down her cheeks. "Oh, Anita," she said. "Now I can have hope that I'll see my child again, too."

At the conference table in her office, Goodwin showed me footage on her cellphone, taken by *The Atlantic*'s film crew, of what happened afterwards. Back at La Posada later that night, Jenri, who had finally begun to be affectionate and boisterous—even playing basketball for a while in the refuge parking lot—had a meltdown. There was a bunk bed in the room, and he was playing on the top bunk, near an overhead fan that was running. One of the sisters came in to ask if there was anything Anita needed, and saw him close to the fan. "No touching," she gently scolded in English.

"No touching," Jenri repeated. "No touching. No touching." It was as if he were stuck in a loop he couldn't get out of. Soon, he was on the bottom bunk crying hysterically. "I want to go back to the jail," he told his stricken mother, switching to

Spanish. "You don't love me. You're not my mom anymore. I don't want to be your son."

According to the American Academy of Pediatrics, separation from parents or caregivers produces anxiety, depression, and post-traumatic stress disorder, with young children the most vulnerable. In the long term, such separations produce far greater likelihoods of chronic illness and severe psychological conditions such as schizophrenia and multiple personality disorder. "It is a form of child abuse," AAP president Colleen Kraft said in a television interview. "We know very young children go on to not develop their speech, not develop their language, not develop their gross and fine motor skills and wind up with development delays."

For Goodwin, the scene in the bedroom at La Posada was one that, by the end of the summer, she had seen played out over and over again. "It's psychological torture to the kids," she told me. "They've been betrayed, they've been abandoned, then they've been treated like they're animals, deprived of sensory perception, without having the comfort of a human touch. It was awful. And I saw it in every case."

She exhaled deeply, her eyes filled with tears. "I don't ever want to have to do that again in my life," she said. "It's fucking miserable."

ANOTHER KIND OF TORTURE

In the weeks after the Sabraw injunction, in spite of multiple delays by the government, hundreds of families were reunified in the Rio Grande Valley alone. Often, the reunifications themselves took place at the Port Isabel Detention Center, where the parents had been held. From there, the families were dropped off together, either at the Humanitarian Respite Center, in downtown McAllen, or at the Basilica of Our Lady of San Juan del Valle, in San Juan. At both locations, they received meals, a place to shower, medical care, clothes, diapers, and toiletries. Volunteers also assisted in calling family members and arranging transportation to destinations across the United States where they would stay until their court date, a process that could take as long as a year.

The woman behind the massive humanitarian effort was Sister Norma Pimentel, a 65-year-old nun who is the director of Catholic Charities of the Rio Grande Valley. When I arrived in mid-July at the nondescript storefront, two blocks from the McAllen bus station, that housed the Humanitarian Respite Center, Pimentel welcomed me at the door. She was dressed as always in a navy blue habit, her wavy gray hair swept back from her face.

She led me on a brief tour. In the largest room, a group of volunteers from a Boston-based chain of preschools was transforming a corner into a children's play-space with a puppet theater, dress-up clothes, colorful ABC rugs, kid-size furniture, and plastic bins of dinosaurs and blocks. Along another wall, babies slept in a row of 20 or so sleeper chairs, cribs, and bassinets, on what looked like it used to be a wooden stage; Pimentel called it the "sleeping baby area." Meanwhile, parents sat on blue plastic chairs with volunteers sitting at folding tables with laptops that had spreadsheets of migrant contact information displayed on the screens.

Elsewhere, in a hallway that doubled as a large pantry-like area, a tween-age volunteer sorted donated baby and toddler clothes by size, putting them into labeled bins. On the other side, in a small dining room, several families who were departing before the official lunchtime sat eating chicken soup and warm tortillas.

An adjoining room had been converted into a patient exam area, staffed by two volunteer doctors. I thought of a recent *Dallas Morning News* story featuring interviews with doctors at the HRC. Now that families were no longer being separated at the border, some were arriving directly from *la hielera*. The doctors said that both children and adults arrived with severe coughs; many had respiratory infections and fevers that had gone untreated in detention. Many babies had severe diaper rashes, a result of far too infrequent diaper changes.

Pimentel led me back to the large room where we'd begun, and pulled two of the blue plastic chairs off to one corner. Inside the new play area, the teal-shirted volunteers were taking selfies with three refugee children. "Since day one [after the court order], we started to see families arriving that had been separated," Pimentel told me. "What we try to do is restore their dignity by the way we care for them and receive them. And the children have a space where they can just be a child again."

The HRC has been open since 2014. Initially, ICE was taking asylum seekers from *la hielera* directly to the bus station. Many of the families didn't have tickets or money; most people wore the same clothes they had crossed the river in. A parishioner at the nearby Sacred Heart Parish saw the disoriented crowd at the bus station and called Pimentel, who drove over at 5 o'clock, right after work, and called the parish priest from the station. "I need to use your parish hall for a couple of days," she told him. He agreed. By the following night, the hall was swarming with volunteers, and dozens of asylum seekers were sleeping on donated cots. The McAllen city attorney arrived to check in on what was happening. "What are you doing here?" Pimentel recalls him asking.

"Restoring human dignity," she replied.

The city ultimately pitched in portable showers and other needed services. The "couple of days" for which Pimentel had asked the parish priest to borrow the hall ultimately became three years, until a local businessman—who also happens to be the county sheriff—offered them the storefront rent-free. Fundraising is underway for a larger, permanent center, which Pimentel hopes will break ground later this year.

The first bus of the morning leaves at six, which means that the families need to be at the station by five. Staff and volunteers arrive at four—there's paid security staff overnight—to prepare breakfast, as well as 300 to 400 sandwiches for the families to take with them. Lunch is always chicken soup and warm tortillas. Sometime between one and five in the afternoon, volunteers get a text from ICE letting them know when the next group will arrive, and approximately how many to expect.

Pimentel has cultivated a positive working relationship with ICE and local and state leaders, which she views as essential for the HRC to fulfill its mission. Until he was recently reassigned, she had coffee periodically with Border Patrol Rio

Grande Valley Sector Chief Manuel Padilla to talk about ideas and concerns, and has hosted tours for the two Senators from Texas, John Cornyn and Ted Cruz. At times, those relationships have drawn criticism from other activists, who see her as excessively accommodating. That was especially true in the early days of family reunifications, when reunited families began to be housed at the San Juan Basilica, where some journalists and activists complained that access to the families was limited at a time of high public interest. (The Diocese said it was protecting their privacy.)

Pimentel can come across as deferential, which may at times fuel those criticisms. Still, I had the impression that her manner, while undoubtedly sincere, is also a form of political calculation. Describing her interactions with Padilla, Cruz, Cornyn, and other public officials with whom she is not necessarily ideologically aligned, she said, "I want to help take the scales from our eyes so that we can answer the question, 'What is God asking us to do?'" She smiled cryptically. "I'm not going to tell you what to do. I'll let you, as a political person, decide if you're doing the right thing—or not. I think it's up to you and God to decide that, but before you do, my job is to make sure that you see what is before you."

Pimentel's family is from Matamoros; she was born in Brownsville, but grew up on both sides of the border. Her father was a mechanic. Her mother stayed home with the kids, sewing their clothes while working as her husband's bookkeeper and accountant. An artist from early childhood, Pimentel studied art at the local university in Brownsville, and applied for architecture school at the University of Texas at Austin. While she was waiting for a response, she met a sister at a Catholic social gathering at a Pizza Hut. She'd only gone for the pizza, but by the time they were finished eating, the sister had invited her to a retreat. Within a year, as a 24-year-old, she moved to the convent, where she still lives 40 years later. There are only four women left; she is the youngest.

The convent was where Pimentel first worked with refugees. It was 1980; then, like now, they came from Central America, fleeing civil wars in Nicaragua, Guatemala, and El Salvador that were underwritten by the United States. At first, families stayed in the convent, living with the sisters until they could connect with their families elsewhere in the country. Later, when the numbers grew larger, the Brownsville diocese opened Casa Oscar Romero, a family shelter. The sisters moved from the convent into the shelter, which ultimately provided temporary shelter to tens of thousands of families. For Pimentel, it was a life-changing experience. "We were with them 24/7," she said. "We heard their stories of how people were being killed. We saw their hands that had no nails because they were tortured."

A lifetime of experience working with Central American refugees makes Pimentel acutely aware of the irony of the present crisis. "The terror of gang violence and domestic violence is another kind of torture," she told me. The MS-13 gang, the subject of so many presidential tweets justifying draconian border policies, was originally started in the United States by paramilitary-linked exiles from Central America, and gained a foothold in El Salvador and elsewhere after anti-immigrant politics led to the mass deportation of Central Americans in the 1990s. Denying asylum to refugees fleeing gang violence and domestic abuse meant denying an entire history of American culpability in the region. "Whole countries are being terrorized by these gangs," Pimentel said. "We need to revisit what political asylum is today, in a way that speaks to today's reality."

Pimentel recounted an episode from her early days at Casa Romero. Sister Juliana García, Pimentel's mentor and the shelter's director, invited her to a sit-in at a Brownsville congressperson's office. It was in protest of U.S. support for repressive governments in El Salvador and Guatemala, and the paramilitary contras in Nicaragua, all of which were responsible for large-scale human rights abuses. The two sisters joined a small group of activists praying and singing. When the building manager called the police, García turned to Pimentel. "We can't both get arrested because somebody has to take care of the house," she said, in Spanish. "So, you tell me: Is it going to be you or me?"

Pimentel looked straight at her older mentor, who was responsible for overseeing all the day-to-day activities at Casa Romero. "I guess it's me," she said. She was arrested along with the other protesters. She was fingerprinted. Police took her mug shot in jail.

"All my life, I had been taught to obey the law," Pimentel told me, sitting in a corner of the HRC almost 40 years later. "At that moment, it was like the law of God and the law of man collided." She whisked a strand of grey hair from her forehead. "I believe that there are defining moments in our lives, when we have to decide who we are," she said. "That was my defining moment."

She glanced down at her phone. Another group of refugees was going to be dropped off soon; she was also due to have lunch with visiting doctors from Stanford. As our conversation came to an end, her thoughts turned back to the present, and the parents who by then had finished with intake and were making their way to lunch. "They share with you the stories of what they're experiencing, and what made them uproot themselves from their country, and risk their lives," she told me. "Then, they get here and find a wall that possibly keeps them from coming in."

For the first time, I detected something other than steadfast equanimity in her expression—a small wrinkling of the brow, a gaze into the distance—that seemed to me to convey a degree of frustration, mixed with tiredness, mixed with recognition of her own limitations: A kind of prayer. "The wall is not just a physical wall," she said, "but this wall of resentment, this wall of 'we don't want you here,' this wall of hatred, this wall of indifference, this wall of 'I don't care who you are.'" She sighed deeply. "Maybe we get so caught up in what we think is right or wrong that it's keeping us away from becoming human, and real, and present to those people that we have before us that God has said, 'Help me. Help my child. Help this family.'"

CLOSING TIME

At 10:50 p.m. on Friday, July 27—the day after the court-imposed deadline for family reunifications—Elisa Filippone was woken by a phone call from an unknown number. Though she seldom picked up such calls even during the daytime, something told her it might be important. On the other line was an employee from the Greyhound Station in downtown Brownsville, a half-block from her house. "'Ma'am, you left your number here," the worker said. "There's a woman that we think we shouldn't let outside. You said that you could help."

For much of the summer, Filippone had been volunteering with the Angry Tías and Abuelas, often heading to one or both of Brownsville's two international bridges to deliver backpacks full of supplies. Earlier in the week, she'd seen a post on the Tías group chat about asylum seekers being dropped off at the bus station by ICE in the middle of the night. For several days, she'd come in the evening, but found no one. Eventually, she'd left her name on a Post-it at the Greyhound desk, just in case someone showed up.

Filippone, a 53-year-old, streetwise native of the Mexican border city of Ciudad Acuña, put on her pants and strapped her gun into its holster—she has a Texas-issued concealed carry permit, and goes to the shooting range most Friday evenings after work. Then, she headed to the station, walking fast in spite of her diminutive stature. She'd only lived in her present house for less than a year—her divorce was about to be finalized—but already several incidents had convinced her that the neighborhood wasn't very safe at night. Her fears were confirmed on the walk over. Outside the station door, police were talking with four men whom she recognized because they sometimes loitered around her property, drinking as early as 9 a.m.

When she arrived at the Greyhound counter, she met Jessica, a 30-year-old mother from Honduras. She had dark skin and indigenous features, and appeared disoriented. Filippone invited her to sit down. She learned that Jessica was traveling to South Carolina to be reunited with her daughter whom she hadn't seen since their second day at *la hielera*. The first night, after they'd crossed the river on a raft with a coyote and turned themselves in to Border Patrol, she'd managed to get two foil blankets, and her daughter had slept curled up in her arms. The next morning, a Border Patrol officer had told her that he was going take her daughter to get "cleaned up," and that she'd be back 30 minutes later. That was a month ago. Now, her daughter was scheduled to be released from ORR custody to a relative on Tuesday, and Jessica's bus was supposed to arrive on Monday. But before all that happened, there was a more immediate problem. Her ticket was for 2 p.m. the following day, and the bus station employees were already in the process of locking the doors for the night.

In Brownsville, there was no place like the Humanitarian Respite Center. For a moment, Filippone wondered why ICE hadn't taken Jessica to the HRC, or to La Posada, in San Benito. Then again, after a summer volunteering with the Tías, Filippone had grown inured to new demonstrations of ICE's cruelty or lack of preparation. Probably, she reasoned, it was just that the Greyhound station was a shorter drive back for whichever feckless employee ICE had dispatched to take the young mother off its hands.

As the bus station employees eyed her impatiently, Filippone made a split-second decision: She would do whatever it took to make sure that Jessica's basic needs of food, shelter, and safety were met. That said, the first night she'd gone to the station, she had made a promise to herself that she wouldn't take anyone home herself, since she lived alone. In the meantime, she'd spoken on the phone with several friends with families or roommates who had agreed to house refugees if the need arose. She called all of them, but no one picked up. Then, she called fellow Tía Madeleine Sandefur, who did. Together, they agreed that the Tías would pay for a hotel room for the night.

Filippone and Jessica walked to her house, where they got into her old white pick-up and drove to the hotel. They arranged to meet for breakfast the following morning at 9 a.m. When Filippone arrived, Jessica said she wasn't hungry. They waited together at the bus station. She didn't eat lunch, either, perhaps because she was nervous about the trip ahead, or perhaps, Filippone speculated, because she was sick from the detention center. At last, the bus arrived, and Filippone waved goodbye.

Much later, Filippone would speak to Jessica in South Carolina by phone. She was with her daughter. By then, she was more or less settled. She'd received a work permit to allow her to support her family while she waited on her case. She thanked Filippone, and said she was doing fine.

When I met Elisa Filippone in mid-August at the Brownsville bus station, she showed me briefly around the station, pointing out the ticket counter where she'd first met Jessica, and a gated "yard" in the back with metal benches with bars in the center to deter loiterers—or refugees—from lying down. Sometimes, on nights when ICE dropped off as many as 30 asylum seekers at one time, right before closing, a group still had to stay there. There wasn't room for all of them at the network of houses, apartments, and churches Filippone had cobbled together, although she always made sure that the women, at least, had proper accommodations.

Filippone invited me to walk back with her to her house a half-block away, where she opened a padlock on a gate with a large No Trespassing sign in two languages. We sat down next to a sunning cat on the porch of the 127-year-old house that she moved into in the spring, after she and her husband, an engineer at a *maquiladora* factory across the border in Matamoros, made the mutual decision to divorce.

Before she'd moved in, there hadn't been a fence, and she believed the property had been a meeting place for heroin addicts, since she'd found used syringes all over the yard. But now, with the youngest of her three children in college, she was fixing up the once-dilapidated house and the historic building next door, which had once been Brownsville's first department store called *El Globo*, or The Globe. The idea was to restore the buildings according to their original blueprints. Eventually, she planned to turn the former department store into townhomes and loft apartments for young professionals, contributing to the rebirth of Brownsville's long-neglected downtown. For the summer, though, the project had gone on hiatus as she became consumed with the family separations.

Over time, as more and more refugees like Jessica appeared at the station, she'd developed a system. They were dropped off anytime between 7 and 11 p.m.; if she showed up at 9 p.m., she could stay for two hours and not miss anyone. The asylum seekers were easy to spot. They carried the same mesh bag issued by the Port Isabel Detention Center, usually their only luggage. She approached the women first, scanning to see if anyone was pregnant. If so, they were her first priority. "¿Ya lo *dejaron salir?*" she asked first, inquiring if they'd just been released in her melodic border Spanish. "Of course, they don't know me," Filippone told me. "They probably shouldn't trust me. But they're in such a tough spot. What are they going to do?" She offered them one of her backpacks to replace the mesh bag. After they accepted, she asked about the ticket. Once that was arranged, then they'd worry about housing. At first, Filippone relied just on friends and acquaintances who had spare bedrooms—a fellow book club member, a member of the Frontera Progressives, a *Neta RGV* editor, the parents of one of her daughter's theater troupe friends.

For more than a month, Filippone ran the entire operation by herself. Eventually, though, other volunteers began to pitch in and help. Becky and Eduardo Argüelles, a young couple who owned an art studio on the corner near Filippone's house, saw her being interviewed by *Neta RGV* on Facebook. They asked if they could help, and Filippone invited them to go with her to the bus station one evening. They began helping Filippone two nights a week, and eventually convinced their Seventh Day Adventist church to host larger groups on cots in the sanctuary. Church members, many of them relatives, took turns staying up nights to provide security. The group decided to call themselves the Primos, in keeping with the family theme started by the Tías.

Later, Filippone helped me catch up with Becky Argüelles at City Hall, where she was in the process of applying for a permit for a new, larger studio building a few blocks away. A petite, introverted painter who has lived in Brownsville her entire life, Argüelles said that she had been initially apprehensive about approaching strangers, mainly because she was nervous about what to say. "I didn't want to say anything that might offend them or make them feel bad," she told me. "I was very conscious about what I'd say, how I'd dress, what my body language would convey to them." After the first few times, she told me, she'd gotten used to it. She no longer felt anxious approaching a total stranger.

The name Primos, which the group put on bright red T-shirts that they wear to the station, stems in part from the fact that many of the volunteers are, in fact, cousins—or at least related in some way. But it also holds another meaning, Argüelles said. "It's a cultural thing," she told me. "Down here, even though I don't know you, I might start a conversation with, 'Eh, primo—'" The word for cousin in the Rio Grande Valley is also a term of address for a total stranger, a kind of linguistic reminder that we're all related somehow. "You can call anybody primo," Argüelles explained.

The Primos helped lighten Filippone's load, as did several new Tías from Brownsville, who'd also taken over some nights. One such volunteer Filippone had come to rely on was Sergio Córdova. As it turned out, I'd met him before. In June, I covered a Families Belong Together rally at the Brownsville federal courthouse. Twelve hundred people had attended the rally, but Córdova stood out from the crowd in his Dallas Cowboys jersey beneath an olive jacket on which he'd painted "All Decent Human Beings Care"—a not-so-subtle reference to the controversial jacket Melania Trump had recently worn on her way to visit a children's shelter in McAllen. He and a friend were holding poles at either end of a homemade clothesline. Hanging from clothespins were white onesies, each with one letter scrawled out in permanent marker: R-E-U-N-I-T-E.

A few days after Córdova started volunteering at the bus station, Filippone recounted, he asked about changing the name of the group. "It has to be Tíos and Abuelos," he said, since in Spanish the masculine -os plural is traditionally used to describe groups consisting of members of both genders.

"Hold on," Filippone replied, with characteristically acerbic wit. "You're a Tío. Are you happy to be a Tío?" He'd nodded sheepishly, perhaps knowing already where she was headed. "Now," she continued, "changing the name? When we stop saying mankind, when we have affordable childcare, when we have equal pay, when we acknowledge the fact that the right to abortion is a health issue and not a moral issue—when we do all that, then we'll talk."

Actually, though, Filippone told me on her porch that she didn't even consider herself to be a Tía. Not because she wasn't a valued member of the core team—she was—but because she was painfully aware that no matter how much time and effort she devoted to the group, there was always more to be done.

"Well, you can aspire to be a Tía," she told Córdova. "I aspire to be a Tía, too. I'm just not there yet."

SWITCHING SIDES

Laura Peña was scrolling through Facebook at the Phoenix airport, on her way back to California from a friend's June wedding, when she came across a livestream of Texas Civil Rights Project lawyer Efrén Olivares, who had been going to the McAllen courthouse every day for over a month by then, giving a speech at a protest outside *la hielera*. She was riveted. For one thing, Peña was deeply knowledgeable about the issues he was speaking about. During the first term of the Obama administration, she had worked as a special advisor to Secretary of State Hillary Clinton with a focus on democracy and human rights in Central America, and had traveled extensively in the region. Then, after completing her law degree at night at Georgetown, she'd accepted a job in California working as an ICE prosecutor.

But there was also another reason that Peña couldn't turn her eyes away from the screen on her phone. For Peña, the Rio Grande Valley is also the home she had left nearly two decades earlier.

"When this crisis hit, I just knew I needed to come home and be a part of it," Peña told me, when we spoke in her office at the TCRP in Alamo, where the only decorations were her law degree on the wall and stacks of thick immigration law books. Peña, 36, has long brown hair and wears tortoise-rim glasses, and speaks in conversation with a disarming half-whisper that draws listeners forward in their chair.

"I felt called to do this work, in a true sense of the word," she said. Like many high-achieving members of her generation raised in this part of the country, she'd left for college and never returned. That put her in good company, statistically speaking. For decades, the Rio Grande Valley has experienced an extensive brain drain. Partly as a result, the two largest communities, McAllen and Brownsville, have the third and second lowest median income in the country, respectively, and less than one in five area residents holds a bachelor's degree.

Peña was born in McAllen, and grew up in Harlingen, where she was a drum major in high school. She comes from one of the most politically connected families in the Rio Grande Valley. Her uncle was a judge—the Brownsville federal courthouse is named for him—and her cousin is Filemón Vela, the U.S. congressman from Brownsville whose simmering anger about injustice on the border boiled over in an open letter to the President that concluded, "Mr. Trump, you're a racist, and you can take your border wall and shove it up your ass." Peña got her first taste of politics as a summer intern, after her first year at Wellesley College, in the office of Blanca Vela, the first female mayor of Brownsville, and also her aunt.

Near the end of the Obama administration, Peña had left ICE, and gone to work in Silicon Valley as a business immigration attorney, helping employees at companies like Google and Apple with their immigration paperwork. She'd already been contemplating a move home when she saw Olivares's speech. She quickly emailed him from the Phoenix airport. As it turned out, he had just received approval for a temporary fellowship that would double the number of lawyers in the office, from one to two. Days later, she was on a flight home. She moved in with her parents. "Thirty-six years old, living with my parents." She laughed, before adding, "You know, I'm actually enjoying it. Our parents aren't going to be around forever."

Before she left, she penned an op-ed for *USA Today* that ran under the headline "Former ICE Lawyer Switches Sides." She wrote:

> I became a lawyer because I believe in the rule of law and fundamental fairness, not to prosecute babies and send them traveling in planes alone. As our government cracks down on asylum-seeking families, we are witnessing mass violations of constitutional and international laws that uphold the right to family unity, the protection of asylum seekers from criminal prosecution, and the rights of children to live free from harm.

As a new lawyer, she hadn't exactly set her sights on prosecuting deportation cases for ICE. But there was a hiring freeze at the time, and the Department of Homeland Security was the only government agency exempt. In spite of her initial reluctance, the experience had given her powerful insight into the inner workings of the government's immigration bureaucracy. And under Obama administration guidelines, she'd had considerable discretion about which cases to prosecute, with priority assigned only to those that involved serious criminal histories.

The zero-tolerance policy had removed that discretion entirely, and made family separation inevitable. When the first migrant crisis began, in 2014, Peña had been brand new on the job. She remembered working meticulously to ensure that families stayed together, marking up case files with red pens and rubber-banding together those involving members of the same family. Now, she was appalled that many of her former colleagues were being asked to do the exact opposite. "I just knew, because I had been part of the system, that this meant that children were going to be orphaned at our doing," she told me. "If we can't abide by our laws, if we can't abide by international law, we're losing who we are as a nation."

On July 9, her first day of work at the Texas Civil Rights Project, Peña found herself squarely in the middle of a crisis. Even after the June 20 executive order, TCRP staff had continued to interview asylum seekers at the McAllen courthouse. While parents were apparently no longer being separated, they recorded the names and dates of birth of other separated family members—aunts, uncles, grandparents, cousins—who were sometimes a child's only guardian. While those relatives had no legal basis for reunification, TCRP could at least facilitate a phone connection. They didn't expect to come across any more parents.

But that morning a TCRP law clerk interviewed Mario, a distraught Guatemalan man who spoke primarily Mam, an indigenous language. If the clerk had understood correctly—the language barrier made communication difficult—the story she heard was alarming. At *la hielera*, a Border Patrol agent had told Mario that he thought the birth certificate he'd brought with him was fake, and that his two-year-old daughter wasn't actually his daughter. Nearly three weeks after the executive order, Mario and his daughter were separated.

Peña met with Mario at the Willacy County Regional Detention Center, a smaller facility outside rural Raymondville. By that time, his daughter had already been sent to an ORR shelter in El Paso, 750 miles away. He was terrified and despondent. Right away, Peña found major flaws in the government's handling of the case. They hadn't found a Mam translator, nor had they checked with the Guatemalan consulate in McAllen to verify the validity of the birth certificate.

At the TCRP office in Alamo, Peña and Olivares discussed how best to proceed. It was *possible*, of course, that the government was correct. But Mario frantically insisted that he was the girl's father, and both lawyers were far more inclined to believe the word of a clearly traumatized father than that of a government which as recently as June had lied about the very existence of a family separation policy. Still, the lawyers did what due diligence was possible, including a preliminary check with the Guatemalan consulate. When the birth certificate checked out as authentic, on July 13, they decided to go to the press.

Meanwhile, Peña visited Mario at Port Isabel, where he had been transferred, and negotiated on his behalf with the government to get a DNA test. That took a couple of weeks. At last, nearly a month after Mario was separated from his two-year-old, the results came back. He was the father.

ICE flew his daughter from El Paso, and they were reunified at the San Juan Basilica.

For Peña and Olivares, the lesson was clear. "That was a stark reminder that we need to continue going to court," Olivares told me, in August. "The government acted just on a hunch—and no one has been held accountable."

The TCRP has committed to reunifying every one of the 382 parents they interviewed at the courthouse, as well as to finding them pro bono legal representation for their asylum cases. As of the end of September, they were still working closely with the cases of 12 separated parents. Peña was constantly on the phone, talking to detained parents, consulting with the pro bono lawyers, and trying to get information from the government. "It's really like reading tea leaves in terms of figuring out why the government decides to do a reunification, or why it's dragging its feet," Peña said.

If the government has raised objections related to criminal history or parentage, TCRP talks with family members, the consulate, and the public defenders, and then sends the information it finds to the ACLU, which represents the separated parents covered under the Sabraw injunction. In August, the government argued in court filings that it was the ACLU and its nonprofit partners, like the TCRP, who were ultimately responsible for reunifying the remaining children with their parents. Judge Sabraw deemed this contention "unacceptable," since family separations were "100 percent the responsibility of the administration."

The TCRP is partnering with Justice in Motion, a nonprofit network of human rights defenders that works across Central America, to track down parents deported to Central America without their children. The task is complicated by the fact that many are trying to hide from the same violence they fled in the first place. Scores of addresses listed in a government database shared with the ACLU and its partners are meaningless. Some list *calle sin nombre* or "street without a name," while others have the address of a detention facility in the United States.

Meanwhile, Peña, Olivares, and the rest of the TCRP staff try to celebrate the victories along the way to help them sustain the energy to keep fighting. One particularly gratifying moment for Peña was the reunification of Vilma, the first named petitioner in the complaint the TCRP submitted to the Inter-American Commission on Human Rights. In her first weeks at the nonprofit, Peña had worked closely with Vilma and her pro bono attorney to secure her bond in Washington state. Ultimately, she flew to Houston to be reunited with her 11-year-old son. "She's such an extremely courageous mother," Peña told me. "She didn't work in Guatemala. She was a homemaker. She speaks an indigenous language. But she knew that she wanted her son to have a better opportunity, and she was scared to death his only parent was going to be murdered also."

In August, the TCRP received notice that its request to the Inter-American Commission had been granted. The commission formally condemned the separation of families, and ordered that Vilma and the four other named petitioners be reunited with their children immediately. The decision had taken so long as to have no practical effect, but at least it had sent a clear message: Family separation was illegal under international law.

When we last spoke, Peña was still visiting frequently with two mothers at Port Isabel. Both had been separated from their children for more than three months, and were in a deteriorating state of physical and mental health. One of the mothers told Peña that she had stopped eating. She was depressed, and she wasn't sleeping; she said the food made her feel sick. Her daughter had already been released to family, and her pro bono attorney had just filed an emergency stay of deportation. Peña feared that she might be deported any day. In the meantime, she'd done her best to convince her to keep eating. "These last cases are really tough—all of them," she told me. "I feel responsible to give these parents hope, so they can continue fighting, and have strength for their children."

Daniel Blue Tyx

ROOM AT THE INN

In the dining room at La Posada Providencia, 12 refugees, three elderly Catholic sisters, the shelter's middle-aged director, and I sat down for lunch at two large round tables. The food was prepared by a Honduran cook, a young refugee himself who had recently received his work permit in the mail, allowing him to return to his profession as a chef while his asylum case made its way through court. Served buffet-style in tinfoil casserole dishes laid out on a long rectangular table, the international smorgasbord featured an assortment of beans, lentils, chicken, salads, breads, rice, and fruit prepared in approximation of the various traditions of the nine countries represented in the room—with a more universal dish of unseasoned rice and beans for two toddlers, the pickiest eaters. While asylum seekers from Central America are in the headlines, refugees from other parts of the world, particularly Africa and the former Soviet republics, also continue to arrive to the border, many having made harrowing overland trips across the Americas from as far away as Brazil, where officials were less likely to question fake passports or a lack of entry documents altogether. At the dinner table, English was the lingua franca, although some diners were more fluent than others, making the conversation proceed in fits and starts. Delly, an opposition political activist from Zimbabwe, spoke effortlessly with a British accent. Yesenia, a mother from El Salvador whose four-year-old son, Angel, devoured three plates of rice and beans, mainly listened, but laughed when others at the table complained that one dish was too spicy. "Not for me," she said.

La Posada Providencia translates as the Providence Inn, although it's mainly just La Posada to residents. Since its founding in 1989 by the Sisters of Divine Providence, the shelter has housed asylum seekers in two dorms—Casa Carolina, for women, and Casa Guillermo, for men, both named after the first residents there—in modest wood-framed white buildings with baby blue trim. The grounds are shaded by expansive ebony and live oak branches, and there's a garden, a gazebo, and a screened-in porch. There are two white vans that come and go throughout the day, taking residents to court appointments, and a tall flagpole, around which the residents gather in the mornings to recite the Pledge of Allegiance.

For most of the parents who had arrived since the court injunction, La Posada was a temporary way station, similar to the Humanitarian Respite Center. They made phone calls and travel arrangements, showered, ate, and then one of the three sisters who lived on site—Zita, Thérèse, and Margaret—took them to the bus station. Soon, they would join family members or friends elsewhere in the country to await their court dates. But a few, like Delly, Yesenia, and her son Angel, became long-term residents. They didn't know anyone in the United States. For them, La Posada was the only place to turn.

After lunch was over and the dishes were washed—the residents do all of the cleaning, and I pitched in by babysitting Angel and another toddler while the chores got done—I sat outside under the shade of an oak tree with Delly and Yesenia. While we spoke, Delly, who was eight months pregnant, had another baby swaddled in a brightly patterned cloth tied around her back, slowly falling asleep; he belonged to a mother from the Congo, with whom she'd developed a relationship akin to a *comadre*, or godparent. Meanwhile, the rambunctious Angel played a game of tag with a college student who was volunteering as an English teacher over the summer. While they waited for the afternoon class to begin, the two women discussed their lives. Delly had a deep alto voice that radiated warmth, and a full-bodied laugh that spread infectiously to the other mothers. She told me matter-of-factly, as though relaying the horrors of another woman secondhand, that she had been gang-raped by members of the ruling party before she fled. She had decided to keep the baby. He would, in all likelihood, spend the first few months of his life here, at La Posada.

Yesenia left El Salvador after her husband was shot in the abdomen; the bullet was still lodged between his liver and his ribs. The family's journey had been difficult, she said. Many days only Angel ate. After they crossed the river and turned themselves into Border Patrol, her husband was taken to a different detention center. He was in deportation proceedings, and was scheduled to be returned to El Salvador any day. After many difficult phone calls, she had made the decision to keep fighting her case without him. Perhaps someday, in the still distant future, she could sponsor him. For now, she hoped, at least she and Angel would be safe.

Her husband had been a migrant worker before in Washington state—he had a previous deportation order—but Yesenia had never been to the United States. "I didn't have anyone here who would take me," she said. When she and Angel came to La Posada, the sisters helped her find a lawyer. She felt lucky, because other women, especially those who had arrived more recently, were still navigating their cases on their own.

Yesenia worried constantly about Angel. Before they left El Salvador, he had begun acting aggressively. "Children can't help but be influenced by what's going on around them," she said. Whenever he saw a red shirt, or a shirt with a stain on it, he'd say things like, "This is blood. Blood like the blood that was coming out of my dad."

Recently, one of the sisters had driven the two of them to the nearest school to sign Angel up for Pre-K. The plan was for him to attend school at least until the court case was finished. The sister had bought him a backpack and a new pair of shoes. He was excited, Yesenia said, although he kept saying that he wished that his dad could be there for the big day. Yesenia was excited, too, but also anxious. Even at La Posada, she never let him out of her sight. It was hard for her to contemplate the idea of him being gone for eight hours a day. "He's getting ready for school," she said. "I'm getting myself ready, too."

Since early July, Selma Yznaga, the University of Texas Rio Grande Valley counseling professor who had received the phone call about the upheaval in the courthouse in April, has been making the 40-minute trip from Brownsville two times a week to provide mental healthcare services in the converted shed that doubles as the English classroom during the day. The one-on-one sessions often last far longer than the 45 minutes she'd typically allot to a client in private practice. For the mothers in particular, it could take hours, days, or sometimes weeks before Yznaga felt ready to broach the subject of basic coping strategies, let alone begin to contemplate next steps like court hearings.

When I spoke with Yznaga at her home in Brownsville, she had been to La Posada the previous evening, where she had had a particularly intense session with a mother who had been separated. She described to me a typical session. At first, she said, almost all of the mothers presented clear signs of what Yznaga referred to as dissociation: They hadn't been sleeping. They were disoriented and uncommunicative, almost as if they were mentally impaired in some way. Their bodies were clenched in a constant state of panic. Their faces were blank, expressionless.

"That's scary," Yznaga told me. "Psychologically, if you blank out your emotions, you blank out everything. You don't feel fear and pain and anxiety, but you also don't feel joy, you don't feel hope, you don't feel optimism—and that's what keeps you moving forward."

Yznaga began each session with a folk saying she'd grown up hearing at funerals in the Rio Grande Valley. *Te acompaño en tu dolor*; I accompany you in your pain. Later in life, after years of living in Austin—she eventually moved back home to raise her kids—she had come to appreciate the phrase's implied message of solidarity without judgment or expectation. It struck her as different from expressions she heard up north: Things are going to get better. Time will heal. What can I do to help?

Te acompaño en tu dolor. For Yznaga, it was a way of saying, in fewer words, but in a way she felt confident the mothers would understand: I know how horrible this is for you. I can't change it. There is nothing I can do to put your child back in your arms right now. I will sit with you, and I will be in pain with you, so that you're not here by yourself.

Yznaga thought of the initial stage of this therapy as *desahogando*, another Spanish word which might best be translated into English as catharsis, but whose root words literally mean "undrowning." She encouraged the women to take deep breaths, as though coming up for air. She tried to help them get to the point where they no longer felt the need to keep their composure, or to filter or censor any of the pain they had experienced over the course of their journeys to La Posada.

Yznaga and the mothers frequently went for a walk around the grounds, which she often did as a way to break up the long sessions. The back and forth of therapy receded into silence. The only sound was the rustling of the South Texas wind in the leaves of the ebonies and the live oaks.

That was the moment during her session the previous night, Yznaga said, when she felt like they'd finally made a breakthrough. "Do you realize how unbelievably strong you are to have survived everything you've been through?" Yznaga had asked, sensing an opening in the mother's silent stillness. "Do you realize how strong that makes you?"

"I'm tired of being strong," the mother answered. "I just want to be weak."

At that moment, Yznaga said she saw a physical transformation take place. The young mother's muscles relaxed. Her gaze sharpened, regained focus. Yznaga felt confident enough to begin talking about strategies that might help her in the process of *desahogando*: Deep breaths. Positive self-talk. Reminding herself that, for the moment, she was no longer in physical danger.

Eventually, hours into the session, the two women began to daydream about the future. Not yet about the obstacles ahead—the fear of being blamed for the separation by your own child, and then the court case, and the very real prospect of deportation, the looming specter that everything you have gone through may have been for nothing—but about tangible things. "What color bedspread will you have when you have a room of your own?" Yznaga asked. "What color comforter? Will it be thick or thin?"

Yznaga knew that it might all prove to be wishful thinking. But she also knew that this sort of imagining could be the key to sustaining the emotional fortitude necessary to endure the long process ahead. As a therapist, Yznaga told me that she found it useful to focus on tangible things like the bedspread the mother would one day pick out "instead of letting their minds race and race and *oh my God oh my God oh my God what's next?*"

"Well, this is what's next," she told me that she wanted to convey to the mother. "You're going to have a house. You're going to have a bedroom, where everyone is safe."

EPILOGUE: LA LUCHA CONTINÚA

In August, as the summer of 2018 finally came to an end, I received a phone call while sitting at the dinner table with my wife and kids. It was an unknown number from an area code I didn't recognize, and the first time I ignored it. But when I got another call from the same number a few minutes later, I decided to pick up. A staticky recorded message began to play in Spanish, informing me that it was a call from a detention center. Then, a woman's voice came on the other line. "*Hola*," she said, "*soy Josefina.*"

A week or so earlier, I'd gotten back into touch with Sara Ramey to follow up on what had happened since I'd stepped in as her assistant in June. Much of the news was good, at least for the time being. Most of the parents I'd met that day had since been reunited with their children. But weeks after the final deadline set by the court injunction, Ramey was still trying to reunify three mothers with their children, including Josefina, who was from Honduras.

The connection wasn't good, as if we were speaking to one another from across a large room full of echoes. At times, Josefina's voice cut out altogether. She told me that she had been separated from her four-year-old son, Erik, at the Hidalgo-McAllen international bridge, but that the case was complicated by the fact that she was his adoptive mother. A 51-year-old grandmother of seven, Josefina had cared for Erik since the day he was born, after his biological mother, who was homeless and addicted to drugs, relinquished custody at the hospital. When she arrived at the bridge, Josefina told the Customs and Border Protection officer that she was Erik's mother, in part because she feared that they might take him away, and in part because that's the way she'd always thought of herself: as his mom.

Later, in a follow-up call, Ramey had filled me in on further details about Josefina's case. They had already submitted photos, testimony, and medical records to ICE to prove that Josefina was in fact Erik's sole guardian. Josefina also had traveled with his passport and birth certificate. Now, it wasn't entirely clear if parentage was the issue causing the holdup, or if it was a prior deportation order— Josefina had lived in the United States for a spell before Erik was born, and missed a court date because she'd already voluntarily left the country—or if it was the fact that Erik was already with another family member. A form letter from ICE denying Josefina's request for reunification hadn't given any reason for the decision. Ironically, the fact that Josefina had crossed at a port of entry—the "right" way to apply for asylum, according to the Trump administration—was working against her. In a quirk of the asylum system, only migrants who crossed outside of ports of entry were allowed to appeal to an immigration judge for release on bond.

Months in detention, Josefina told me over the phone, had made her depressed. Her blood pressure had shot up. She'd begun experiencing chest pain, for which she'd received medical care; a sympathetic cardiologist had supplied records in support of her case. Her hair had begun falling out, a condition that was common among the women in her pod. "All of the women here are going bald," she told me in Spanish. She attributed this to the stress, the low-quality shampoo, and the scalding water temperatures. In Honduras, she'd never used hot water to bathe. She had a job cleaning bathrooms and the dining area that paid a dollar a week. "Here," she told me, "you have to humiliate yourself to survive."

Meanwhile, Erik had been released. He was with her daughter Evelyn in Austin, but he was struggling. Evelyn said he frequently had tantrums and acted out of control. She told Josefina that she thought it was better if she didn't speak with her son, because it upset him so much. They'd kept talking, but not as often as Josefina would have liked. During a recent conversation, he had grown angry because he said that he wanted to see his mother through the telephone. When Josefina's daughter showed him a picture instead, he swatted it away. "No!" he screamed. "I don't want it like that!" He started hitting himself and scratching violently at his skin. Josefina's daughter was upset. "You have a very delicate child," she told her mother, "nothing like our own family."

Over the phone, I heard Josefina crying. "He's a beautiful, beautiful little boy," she said. "He's always called me *mamá*. 'The only thing I want is to see you,' he says. 'Why don't you come?'"

By the end of September, around 350 parents remained separated from their children. Most were still in detention. About 100 parents were deported and hadn't yet been located in their home countries. Reunifications were still happening, albeit infrequently. When I called Laura Peña in late September, she texted back that she wasn't able to talk—she was inside the Port Isabel lobby, waiting for the reunification of one of the TCRP's clients, who had been separated from her daughter for five months.

There had been other good news for the Angry Tías of the Rio Grande Valley. On September 13, an agreement was reached with the Department of Justice in response to three different lawsuits over the coercion of separated parents. The agreement covered cases in which the government had pressured parents to abandon their asylum claims in exchange for reunification, as well as those Jodi Goodwin had described to me in which parents were so distressed by the separation that they weren't able to participate fully in the credible-fear interviews. Ultimately, the agreement may grant up to 1,000 parents a second opportunity to present their asylum cases.

Meanwhile, the grassroots organizing that took root during the summer of 2018 hasn't stopped. Mike Seifert and Christina Patiño Houle are preparing to launch a second court watch at the children's immigration court in Harlingen, where children as young as toddlers were asked to present their cases during family separation, sometimes without a lawyer. Central to this effort are dozens of volunteers who got involved over the summer, many of them young professionals of the kind who've historically left the Rio Grande Valley, but have recently started to stay—and return—in larger numbers. The influence of this new generation of activists isn't confined to the court watch. Many were instrumental in a large-scale get-out-the-vote campaign leading up to the 2018 election. Family separation in particular was a galvanizing issue on the border as Texas set new records for voter registration in a non-presidential election year; turnout in the Rio Grande Valley in November ultimately doubled that of the midterm election of 2014.

The Angry Tías and Abuelas continue to stuff backpacks to hand out to asylum seekers at the bridges and bus stations. If anything, the pace of their work has only quickened. In the run-up to the midterms, the Trump administration abruptly released thousands of refugees to bus stations and shelters in a calculated attempt to portray the border region as overwhelmed by asylum seekers. During that time, I received a text from my friend John Garland, the Mennonite pastor with whom I'd traveled to Nuevo Laredo in June. He needed help on the ground in McAllen.

Over the summer, a young Honduran mother named Lucy had stayed a few days at the Mennonite church shelter in San Antonio with her infant daughter. During that time, John and his family had grown close to Lucy. She told them that while she had been reunited with her daughter, her family was still separated because her husband, Martín, and teenage twin sons were in Honduras. They hadn't all been able to afford to make the trip.

Lucy and her daughter were with family members in Virginia waiting for her asylum court date. Eventually, Martín saved enough money to make the trip to rejoin them. But after he and the boys finally reached the border, Lucy lost contact with them. Days passed. Eventually, she called John in San Antonio in the hopes of enlisting his help. He called me, and I agreed to go look for them.

We knew it was a long shot. I checked the bus station first, armed only with a grainy cell phone photo and a name. They weren't there, but a boy about the same age as the twins said he thought he'd met them at *la iglesia*, which I took to mean the Humanitarian Respite Center. In the wake of Trump's mass release, hundreds of refugees filled the entire facility, plus an outside overflow area. Even if the family was actually there, finding them wasn't going to be easy. There was also the chance that they could still be in detention, and the unspeakable possibility of some worse fate.

I quickly found a volunteer on night duty who offered to help. We strode through the inside waiting area first, trying to be heard without waking the sleeping babies. When that didn't work, we headed outside, where groups of refugees were huddled together in the late-evening cold. We were about to give up when I saw two adolescent boys weaving their way through the crowd in our direction. I knew right away it was the twins, not only because of the similarity in their visages, but also because they wore matching clothes. Their father Martín was right behind them.

Their family ended up staying the night at my family's house. The boys ate leftover Halloween candy and played with my kids' Legos. Meanwhile, Martín described their harrowing journey. Traveling without the aid of an expensive *coyote*, or smuggler, they'd managed to make it by train and on foot as far as Tampico, Tamaulipas, about 300 miles south of the border. That's where their good fortune ran out. Corrupt police had demanded to see their papers. When Martín said they had none, he assumed they would be deported. Instead, they were handed over to members of the *Zetas* drug cartel, who told Martín that they would be killed if they didn't supply the names of family members in the United States to demand ransom money from. When Martín refused, they stole his phone and threatened physical harm. Before that could happen, Martin noticed a small window high up in the room where they were held captive. Left alone for a fleeting moment, he and the boys managed to squeeze their slight frames through the opening.

They escaped, but ever since then Martín told me he had been having terrifying nightmares. In his dreams, the *Zetas* were always right behind him, poised to recapture him and punish his family for their flight.

After Martín and the boys finally reached the United States, they were held at *la hielera* for six days. The lights were kept on 24 hours a day. No one slept for more than a few minutes at a time. Finally, on camping mats and sleeping bags on our living room floor, they slept 12 hours straight. In the morning, I dropped off my own kids at school, and returned to make them breakfast. Then it was off to the bus station. From there, they would travel to San Antonio to meet up with John, who would arrange for more bus tickets to Virginia, where Martín would join Lucy in waiting for his court date.

At the station, every bus leaving northward had already sold out; luckily, I had booked tickets online the previous night. Every seat in the large terminal was filled. Dozens of other travelers waited on the floor. It was hard to hear the garbled announcements for arriving and departing buses over the din of crying babies and the general shuffling of bodies and belongings. I had an appointment to make, but was reluctant to leave, fearing that Martín and the twins might miss their bus amid the chaos. Then, I spotted three Tías circulating around the terminal, checking tickets and making sure everyone got on board the correct bus. Two of the volunteers, Susan Law and Elizabeth Cavazos, had been coming to the McAllen bus station since early July, at the height of the family separation crisis. They assured me that they would make sure that Martín and the boys left safely. We stayed talking for a few more minutes, and they reflected on the five months they'd been coming to the station on a daily basis. They told me they kept waiting for the humanitarian crisis to get better. Instead, it kept getting worse.

And still the work of the Angry Tías continues. Meanwhile, the Trump administration continues to erect as many roadblocks as possible for asylum seekers.

Customs and Border Protection has installed toll-like booths at the midpoint of the bridges, alongside a series of orange traffic cones, institutionalizing the practice of making families camp out at the bridge even as the border communities on the Mexican side remain terrorized by cartel violence. Meanwhile, the administration has piloted a plan to make asylum seekers wait in Mexico while their cases wind their way through U.S. immigration courts, forcing them to confront the risks of kidnapping and extortion for months on end, as well as impeding their access to U.S.-based attorneys. Eventually, the administration says it plans to implement the policy across the entire border, although it is being challenged in court.

Finally, the administration has also tried to withdraw from a 1997 agreement known as the Flores Settlement, which limits the amount of time children can spend in immigration detention to 20 days. Instead, the administration wants to detain migrant children and their parents, potentially at military bases, until their cases have been decided. The lower courts have so far denied the government this authority, but the issue could make its way before the Supreme Court. In the meantime, kids are dying in the custody of Border Patrol agents who are ill-equipped to provide basic medical care, let alone respond sensitively to the physical and psychological needs of traumatized detainees. And allegations of sexual and physical abuse, as well as financial improprieties, continue to pile up at the same facilities where the administration would like to see children held for even longer, with even less oversight.

For the present, the Department of Justice policy of removing gang violence and domestic abuse as criteria for asylum is already having a profound impact. In June, the month that Jeff Sessions reversed the decision in *Matter of A-B-*, only 14.7 percent of asylum seekers nationwide passed credible-fear interviews, down from 32.7 percent in June 2017. Overall, asylum denial rates are at a 12-year high. There is a backlog of 750,000 cases, meaning that asylum seekers face waits of months or even years before their cases are heard. For all of their perseverance and suffering, the most likely outcome for parents like Vilma, Andrea, Anita, María, Mario, Delly, Yesenia, Lucy, and Martín is that they will ultimately be deported back to their home countries where they will once again face the same violence they'd attempted to escape.

On September 18, Josefina's asylum claim was heard by an immigration judge. Sara Ramey told the court how Josefina's daughter had been murdered by gang members in Honduras, and presented photographic evidence of scars on Josefina's scalp, arms, and eye, the result of physical abuse by a boyfriend who had also harmed her son Erik. She argued that women who have experienced domestic violence that has been ignored by the police in Honduras should be considered a persecuted group.

The judge denied Josefina's asylum claim.

Josefina plans to appeal, but the judge told her and Ramey that any evidence of gang violence or domestic abuse will not be considered. Meanwhile, her health problems are worsening. If she is ultimately deported, her daughter Evelyn, who works nights at a tortilla factory, will have to save enough money to pay for four-year-old Erik's flight back to Honduras.

The government won't even make sure they get back home together.

APPENDIX: ORGANIZATIONS RESPONDING TO FAMILY SEPARATION IN THE RIO GRANDE VALLEY

Monetary donations to support the grassroots response to the ongoing humanitarian crisis in the Rio Grande Valley and Northern Mexico are always needed and appreciated. In addition, organizations have specific needs for volunteers and donations, some of which are highlighted below. More details about how to donate and get involved can be found at these groups' websites.

ACLU of Texas
https://www.aclutx.org/
Volunteers needed to serve as court watchers, port of entry monitors, and volunteer attorneys.

Angry Tías and Abuelas
www.facebook.com/angrytiasandabuelas
Volunteers needed to assist refugees at the McAllen bus station, as well as deliver supplies to those waiting in Mexico near the international bridges in Reynosa and Matamoros.

Ayudándoles a Triunfar
https://www.facebook.com/AyudandolesaTriunfar/
Seeks donations of tents, sleeping bags, winter clothing, rain ponchos, toiletries, menstrual products, and non-perishable food items.

Catholic Charities of the Rio Grande Valley

http://www.catholiccharitiesrgv.org

Seeks donations of clothes and shoes for all ages, baby supplies, toiletries, sealed snack food, gifts cards for food items, and phone cards. Volunteers are also needed at the Humanitarian Respite Center.

La Posada Providencia

https://lppshelter.org/

Volunteers needed as second language teachers, computer learning assistants, GED instructors, drivers, gardeners and agriculturalists, and receptionists. Also seeks professional volunteers including doctors, nurses, dentists, midwives, optometrists, psychologists and counselors, accountants, and educators.

Migrant Center for Human Rights

https://migrantcenter.org/

Provides support and training for lawyers interested in taking on asylum cases nationwide, as well as volunteer opportunities and internships for law students, translators and interpreters, and mental health professionals. Remote opportunities available. The Center also has a visitation and pen pal correspondence program to support detained asylum seekers.

Texas Civil Rights Project

https://texascivilrightsproject.org/

Seeks bilingual lawyers and law firms interested in representing clients applying for asylum, law clerks, and volunteers to work as translators, community advocates, and fundraisers in the Rio Grande Valley and Austin offices.

CPSIA information can be obtained
at www.ICGtesting.com
Printed in the USA
LVHW022303040819
626504LV00002B/183/P